GÖRAN ANDERSSON

MARSTRAND'S SAILING CHAMPION

AND ENTREPRENEUR

GÖRAN ANDERSSON

MARSTRAND'S SAILING CHAMPION

AND ENTREPRENEUR

BJÖRN ÖRTENDAHL

First published in Swedish in 2019 by Marstrands Hembygdsförening (Marstrand Local Heritage Society) under the title: *Göran Andersson – Marstrands absolut bäste seglare och ung entreprenör!*

Copyright 2019 © Björn Örtendahl

English edition designed and published 2020 by Robert Deaves on behalf of Marstrands Hembygdsförening
www.robertdeaves.uk

All rights reserved

ISBN: 978-1-912724-20-8

All rights reserved. No part of this publication may be reproduced, stored in a retrieval system or transmitted in any form by any means, electronic, mechanical, photocopying, recording or otherwise without the prior written permission of the publisher, the author and any other copyright holders.

CONTENTS

Preface	7
Introduction	9

PART 1 - EARLY YEARS

Raised in Marstrand, schooling and a great interest in sports	11
High school degree and first job	12
Great interest in sports	15
Marstrand Ice Hockey Club, MIK	15
Military service and first job in the marine industry	16
Sailing as a tradition in Marstrand	19
Early 1950s, sailing with paddle boats on Koön	20

PART 2 - SAILING

Emergence of modern dinghy sailing in Marstrand	23
The Finn, designed by Rickard Sarby for the 1952 Olympic Games in Finland	26
Olympics in Rome 1960 and Mexico 1968	29
Races to remember	32
The road to becoming a prominent Finn sailor	33
World Championship in the Finn - Finn Gold Cup	34
OK Dinghy	35
OK Dinghy sailing	36
Marstrand Yacht Club (MSS)	41
Honorary gift, awards, letters and Christmas cards	43
The biggest thing that happened to Göran in the sailing world	45
Fantastic stories: a visit to the king of Thailand	47
More events that must not be forgotten	50
The stay in France and journey home from Bordeaux	51
Snus delivery	52
Göran on training with sailors double booked for a wedding	52
Sailing with Pehr G Gyllenhammar	54

Driving both in Sweden and abroad 55
Books inspired by Göran's sailing successes 55

PART 3 – ENTREPRENEUR
The Marinex company 57
Kits for Optimists 25
Mast production for dinghies 59
Marinex Sailing School 62
Sail production and sail lofts 62
Town hall is the next stop for sail loft 64
New construction on Koön 65
Manufacture of Optimists and OK Dinghies 69
Development of sail production
  and of products for sailors, the invention of a new marine cleat 69
Products for boat manufacturers and sailors 71
Marketing and advertising 74
Marinex established in Australia and New Zealand 75
One of Sweden's leading sailmakers 77
A customer who sailed longer than most 79
Travel to the USA, shopping and holidays 80
Cake on Fridays 82
Sale of Marinex 82
Göran's continued professional life 83
Many heroes behind Göran's results 83
Final words 84

The sinking of the vessel 'Agro Mayor', 22 September 1969,
  west of the small island of Hamneskär 85
The author's closing words 88
Thanks 89

SOURCES REFERENCES AND FACTS
Appendix I - Summary of all of Göran's various great successes in sailing 91
Appendix II - Weather changes, tactics and currents 92

Swedish Sailing Hall of Fame 96
Postscript by the publisher 98

PREFACE

MARSTRAND LOCAL HERITAGE SOCIETY (Marstrands Hembygdsförening) has on various occasions both in writing, and through photos and exhibitions, described historical events and people in Marstrand. The board discussed how we could continue to work on other similar projects in different ways. A name that then for obvious reasons appeared was Göran Andersson's. His importance to sailing, both in Marstrand, as well as internationally, has been very great. Already at a very young age, Göran became known as an entrepreneur in sailmaking and mast building. He started Marinex, a company that was prominent for several years, especially for employment in Marstrand, both for younger and older people.

The undersigned then took on the task of interviewing Göran and at the same time writing down some notes for possible publication, a task that became increasingly larger and more interesting than intended. I would like to say that I have seldom experienced anything more exciting and extensive to tackle and explore. The reason for this is that Göran has experienced so many events that must not be forgotten and which at the same time describe both Göran as a person and a sailor, as well as the development of sailing and the marine industry. His stories, various events and phenomena have stimulated my joy of discovery.

The interest in investigating and penetrating deeper has motivated many hours of work. Reading through previously written material, searching online and making contact with the people involved has been exciting.

Marstrand, spring 2019
Björn Örtendahl

INTRODUCTION

THE FIRST STEP BEFORE MEETING Göran was to interview Sture Andersson, also a very prominent sailor. Sture is Göran's younger brother and my closest neighbour. This was an initial step to get some input and background knowledge before the conversations with Göran. After that, for just over two years, on a number of occasions I went to Göran's home on Skärhamn, to learn about his sailing and business life.

I gained access to a goldmine in the form of an extensive collection of binders with newspaper clippings, photos, thank you letters, correspondence, Christmas cards and much more from all around the world.

Göran also has a prize collection that is completely unique. Much research has been carried out both online and in various journals and books as well as in old yearbooks from the Marstrand Yacht Club (MSS - Marstrands Segelsällskap). In some cases, I have also contacted people who have given me opportunities to have various events described in a broader perspective and from the point of view of each informant.

PART I

EARLY YEARS

RAISED IN MARSTRAND
SCHOOLING AND A GREAT INTEREST IN SPORTS

GÖRAN ANDERSSON WAS BORN ON October 4, 1939 when the family was then living in Lysekil, to the north of Marstrand. In 1946, they moved to Uddevalla and at this time Göran was six years old.

In Uddevalla he has one of his very first memories of being on the water, but it was without a sail. In Uddevalla, there was a lot of urban construction and development in the 1940s, such as HSB houses, shops and schools. Sometimes there was very high water in the Bäveån. During one of these floods, Göran and his friends built vessels from leftover building material, which they moved around in the half-metre-high water. His early interest in being on the water started then.

Göran's father, Thore Andersson, got a job at Göteborgs Bank in Marstrand in the summer of 1950. During that summer, Thore commuted from

The whole Andersson family in 1951. From left: Margareta, Thore, Göran, Anna-Stina, Aina and Sture

the family's wooden shed at the summer residence in Lysekil to the bank. During the week he lived at Andrén's boarding house in Marstrand. The house move load thus went directly from Uddevalla to Marstrand, but the rest of the family spent the summer in Lysekil.

So, the Andersson family came with four children by steamboat from Lysekil to Marstrand in August 1950, where the family settled at Kyrkogatan 29. The day after they arrived, Göran started school in fifth grade and his little brother Sture started in the first grade. One of Göran's earliest memories is that he quickly became friends with Rolf Jitzmark at school. From him he got a cat, which everyone in the family became very fond of.

HIGH SCHOOL DEGREE AND FIRST JOB

AFTER TWO YEARS at Marstrand's school, Göran started in 1953 at Kungälvs Läroverk, where he graduated in 1956 with a high school degree. When Göran got off the bus in Marstrand with his graduation cap on, he was asked by Paul Christensson if he could start working in the fishing port. Göran wondered when they wanted him to start and then he got the answer: "On Monday." So there was no summer vacation for him. Already on Monday he was in place and had to start work. Washing the floor was his first task. Then it was time to learn to count quickly and develop the ability for mental arithmetic.

Göran had no major plans for work and the future when he took his high school degree. The offer he received as a 16 year old was entry into a long and varied working life.

After his first job at the fishing port, Göran was offered a job working for the Danish company, Iver Christensen Trålbinderi (a trawl net manufacturer). The company was large in Denmark at Esbjerg and Ska-

Above: The job at the trawl net company in 1960. Göran on the left. Standing farthest to the right Lennart Rasmusson, kneeling in front of him Bernt Olsson
Below: On board the fishing boat Arkö around 1958

gen and also had a branch in Marstrand. Göran's first duties were to help the Dane, Fritz Jacobsen, do the invoicing.

Fritz had a great interest in sports, as did Göran. They watched the speedway together. There were common points of contact and it was not long before Göran was given extended tasks, such as going to the east coast to take orders for trawls. To gain knowledge and understanding of how fishing was conducted on the east coast, off Öland, Göran had to go out to sea and take part in trawling for herring. He was allowed to accompany the trawler 'Eliana' with the designation VK 53 (VK = Västervik). At this time, trawls were made of cotton and impregnated with cuprinol for longer life, so rather heavy stuff. Göran also got to try out fishing on the west coast in 1958 with the fishing boat 'Arkö', owned by Evert Pettersson on Dyrön, who fished at Fladen. Here Göran remembers how someone thought that the 'boy' should grow up and try snuff. Göran slipped away like a rat but was caught and was given a pinch of snuff, but he never tried it again in the future.

Another memory that Göran remembers from fishing with 'Arkö' was when the famous Swedish boxer Ingemar Johansson was to meet the American, Eddie Machen, on September 14, 1958. After the catch was unloaded in Skagen, it was full speed towards Gothenburg's fishing port. Göran jumped ashore without even taking the rope with him. He took a taxi to Ullevi, and with ticket in his hand found his place at the end of row (together with about 53,600 other spectators – a record for a Swedish sports arena). Göran had to borrow a pair of binoculars from some men who had fortified themselves with alcohol.

Göran with (from left) Leif Enarsson, Rolf Jitzmark and Jan Skyberg

He watched the boxing match for 2.16 minutes, until Ingemar knocked out his opponent. Göran thanked them for the loan; the old men did not even have time to see what happened until it was over.

Göran referees an ice hockey match at Kungsplan sometime in the 1960s

GREAT INTEREST IN SPORTS

GÖRAN WAS ALREADY interested in sports in his early years. As a young man, he had walls full of clippings of various athletes from the Rekordmagasinet magazine, a very common sight among young people interested in sports in the 1950s. One of the idols was Gert Fredriksson, one of the best canoeists of all time.

Table tennis became a sport in the 1950s, which was practiced by many young people in Marstrand. In 1952 a club was formed there as well. From the beginning, they only had a simple table, a slab of wood that was placed on a few trestles. A few years later, they acquired six real table tennis tables and the club was affiliated with the Swedish Table Tennis Association and played in a district series. There were matches in, among other places, the Exercishuset, a gym in Gothenburg. Some of the players were Göran Andersson, Leif Enarsson, Jan Schyberg (Pillo), Rolf Jitzmark (later tennis) and others. Parents and the elderly who were involved in, and supported the club's local structure included Gösta Kristensson, Viking Karle and Rolf Nicander. MSS had a table tennis section, of which Göran was chairman for several years. Göran still plays table tennis once a week. The interest never goes away.

MARSTRAND ICE HOCKEY CLUB, MIK

ON THE TENNIS court up by the Carlstens fortress a number of young people built an ice hockey rink with leftover packaging material from

Marstrand's Mechanical Workshop. It was difficult to get acceptable ice, but at some point a match was played against boys from Kungälv. At one time, Håkan Larsson was the goalkeeper, wearing boxing gloves. This time however it was raining, so the whole rink could not be used. When flushing, you sometimes had problems with air bubbles. Later they moved down to the open area at Badhusplan, where hockey was played for a number of years. Göran was the prime mover in these early hockey adventures. The hockey rink was later taken over by Marstrand Local Heritage Society, who set it up at Myren.

According to Göran, there was a very nice community among the young people in all the sports he practiced as a young man. As an example, he mentions, when fresh water was washed on the salt water ice outside the quay at Widells, or when the snow on the water pond was shovelled off for skating. Just think what a job it was to carry out all the heavy gear to get some skating. According to Göran, Marstrand was a positive place for young people to grow up in the 1950s.

Football was not something Göran showed great interest in, despite the fact that many people kicked the ball in Marstrand during this time. Possibly Göran was a goalkeeper at some point.

MILITARY SERVICE AND FIRST JOB IN THE MARINE INDUSTRY

GÖRAN CARRIED OUT his military service from 1960-61, a total of 340 days in the Navy. He was already established as a sailor and was given a lot of leave to participate in various regattas in Sweden and abroad. A friend in the military service, Hasse Hansson, Rörö, helped Göran to drive a boat and trailer to the fleet area (near the frigate Göran was stationed on), so that his Finn dinghy was ready and in place to be loaded and picked up quickly during training. Before and during the 1960 Olympics in Rome, Göran had a total leave of absence of about 100 days.

After working at the trawl net manufacturer, Göran started working as a 'consultant with his own company', on a commission basis for the company called Västkustbåtar (Torsten Thorsell Viktoriagatan 3, Gothenburg), which in Stenungsund had a number of J14 Långedrags-jullar built (west coast wooden sailboats). Karl Johansson, of Stenungsunds Båtvarv, built about 20 J14s in the 1950s and 1960s, all designed by Tage Hellman.

For health reasons, Västkustbåtar (West Coast Boats) was closed down and Göran, as mentioned previously, started his own business. His new business, Marinex, happened to have the same lawyer as West Coast

Gösta Johansson, Kungsviken

Boats. This meant that the situation that arose was resolved in a good way. The lawyer was Gunne Dellborg and he was also a sailor. There is nothing wrong, according to Göran, to have a lawyer who understood both sailing and business law. Göran realised early on that it was important to get outside help from competent people. With the lawyer's help, he was thus given the opportunity to take over parts of the business, but it was not entirely without problems.

It was not possible for Göran to take a loan from the local bank, because his father, Thore, worked there. He was a chief accountant and according to Göran there was a risk of a dispute if he or Marinex would borrow money there. When Göran at some point later had to pay salaries, he was also not allowed to borrow money from the bank. He solved this instead by borrowing from his grandfather.

About 14 skiffs were delivered to Marinex, with Göran as 'dealer'. Marinex, as a sole proprietorship, already existed then, because he has already hired a carpenter to start manufacturing masts in Kungälvs Ytterby. Göran sold different types of boats, and gigs to, among others, Hoffman, 'Borås-Skoglund'. The company also sold open Bohus skiffs. These were supplied by Halvard Olsson and Gustav Johansson in Henån. [Bohus county, or Bohuslän, is the province of Sweden where Marstrand is located.]

In Fiskebäckskil, converted folkboats were made of mahogany by Salomonson's shipyard, which Göran also sold. Kalle Kristoffersson in Marstrand had employed an Estonian, who built GKSS dinghies. Gustav Eklund's boatbuilding on Köpstadsö (Kössö) also built GKSS dinghies and in several cases Göran was also involved in these deals. At that time, Bengt Palmqvist lived on Kössö, a very famous Dragon sailor, whom Göran had got to know. Palmqvist competed in the Dragon class at the 1956, 1960 and 1968 Olympics. Göran possessed a great ability to create contacts at a very young age, which provided many business opportunities.

A truly exceptional business event must also be mentioned to demonstrate his ability, to execute an odd sale and delivery.

One day an American came into Göran's office, located in the former Svalanders Kaffehandel (a coffee retailer), which was located by the park next to the church. It was a priest from the Mississippi Delta, in the United States, who was on vacation in Sweden and Marstrand. He started asking questions about a 'fishing boat made of wood'. It was to be built as Göran perceived it, a traditional Bohuslän fishing skiff. After the meeting, Göran called the well-known boat builder Gösta Johansson in Kungsviken, told him that he had a possible buyer of a boat of this type. Göran asked: "*May we come and visit?*" And off they went. When they arrived there, Gösta's wife had been baking, removed all the sheets that covered the furniture in the drawing room, and served coffee and cake. The conversation started with Göran as interpreter. The priest became enthusiastic and wanted to order it immediately. They agreed that construction would begin in the autumn with delivery in two years. The priest made a down payment on the boat, which amounted to one third of the boat's price. When it was completed, the skiff was sent with a Swedish American Line ship to the USA, complete with a mast and a cotton sail. Göran had these sails made at home in Arne Johansson's basement. Arne was the father of Björn Arnesson.

Most Marstrand residents have a number of times ridden as passengers on one of Gösta Johansson's most famous and often photographed creations, namely the electrically powered 'Hamnfärjan II', more commonly known as 'Spårvagnen'. He built it in 1948 and the ferry was in service until June 1985. During this time, the ferry managed to transport about eight million passengers. The last tour was run by Stig Christoffersson, who was also the long time chairman of Marstrand Local Heritage Society. The association 'Färjans Vänner' (Friends of the Ferry) still runs and cares for it today and the ferry is now also K-marked, which means that it has a certain protection and cannot be changed.

(Anyone who wants to read more about Gösta Johansson shipyards and other boat builders on Orust is recommended to read 'Boatbuilders on Orust' by Margareta Bremertz and Eva Borge, Votum publisher ISBN 978-91-88435-09-5.)

The Marinex era is described in more detail later in this book.

Göran in Långedragsekan L 13

Sailing as a tradition in Marstrand

ACCORDING TO OLD Bohuslän tradition, the coastal population sailed various skiffs. These can be said to be heavier and older predecessors to today's dinghies. Marstrand and Klöverö residents sailed mainly J14, J18 and J22. The Bohus Regatta (Bohusregattan) was organised at midsummer time in various places in Bohuslän and famous Marstrand residents such as Båysen, Hellman, Nicander, Lückner and Heijel participated in this regatta.

For a few years in the 1950s, MSS had a lottery in which the prize was one Långedragsekan, colloquially called an L-dinghy. It was designed in 1952 by Tage Hellman, chief designer at Eriksberg's shipyard. He had also designed J14, J18, and J22s.

The L-dinghy was delivered to MSS unpainted and without primer. Some of the MSS juniors were appointed sponsors. This assignment included painting the bottom, painting the oak and also caring for and sailing it until the lottery was completed. Göran was one of the young people who during the summer of 1953 was allowed to perform this

Vitvingepokalen, The White Wing Cup

work on L-dinghy no. 13. The dinghy was won by Gösta Olsson, who named it 'Maggan' after his daughter Margareta. The L-dinghy was initially built in pine and equipped with a sail, spruce mast and centreboard. It was raced diligently for a few years. Margareta remembers, on my question, that her father liked to lacquer and paint it, but it was Göran who used it. After a while, Göran bought the dinghy for about SEK 600 and sailed it successfully with Göran Dahlström as crew.

The boat was named 'Babba'. Göran chose the name after his sponsor, Barbro Asserman, who had the nickname Babba. After L-dinghy no. 13 he sailed L-dinghy no. 55.

The White-Winged Cup (Vitvingepokalen) was a great regatta for L-dinghies with a nice prize. Göran won this prize forever through his three wins, first in 1953, then in 1956 and finally in 1957 (after achieving three wins, a sailor can keep the prize forever). Many families and especially young people in Marstrand enthusiastically sailed these dinghies during the 1950s. The Båysen, Evert Wångdahl, Kristensson, Carl-Axel and Sten Hellman families (L 27). Also, Greger Kristiansson et al. can be mentioned. It is obvious that it was here that Göran's great interest in sailing really took off.

Early 1950s, sailing with paddle boats on Koön

THE FIRST CASUAL sailing most young people did on Koön (the larger of the two islands where Marstrand is located) was when they sailed with 'paddle boats' in Muskeviken and Blekebukta. These were simple flat-bottomed boats that you built yourself from boards and masonite, with masts made from sticks.

Paddle boat in Muskeviken. At the helm is Bo Enarsson

Commander Robert Krusell, a resident of Fredrik Bagges gata / Slottsgatan, supported the boys in this and encouraged them so that they also raced, and he made sure the guys got prizes. There are, even today, preserved result slips from Blekevikens Segelsällskap's weekly racing. The shopkeeper, Lindqvist, photographed the boys' sailing, though unfortunately there are no pictures from these occasions. Göran also built a 'paddle boat' even though he lived on Marstrandsön.

Model paddle boat, belonging to Leif Enarsson

The construction took place outdoors in the garden at the family's home and near the school hall that was on the same property. Göran tried to calculate how much wood was needed (the bottom was of masonite). The calculations went a little awry when some of the boards became too short and he was forced to splice. These joints leaked a lot when the paddle boat was launched and later Göran halted the project. He stated laconically: "*Nothing happened.*"

This sailing on Koön was arguably a good introduction to many of the successes that several of these young people had in their future sailing lives. Even though Göran was not active in these particular exercises, several of the other young people who sailed here came to work with Göran at Marinex in the future.

In 2018, construction of a new paddle boat took place, but only as a model. Leif Enarsson created this nice little boat, and he did so to honour the memory of Bertil Nicander, who passed away some time ago. It was his way of honouring his good friend. They built their own paddle boat together, back in the 1950s.

PART 2

SAILING

EMERGENCE OF MODERN DINGHY SAILING IN MARSTRAND

THE LÜCKNER BROTHERS, Gunnar and Sture, were early pioneers in Finn sailing in Marstrand. Sture had several Finns, S36 and S111. The brothers bought 'baked' boats from England (a construction method where veneer is glued crosswise over a template). They were very skilled and also sailed the Flying Dutchman.

On one occasion, they invited talented Danish and Norwegian Finn sailors, including the Dane, Paul Elvstrøm. Paul was born in 1928, thus he was 11 years older than Göran, and had great sailing successes early on becoming Olympic champion several times, and was the first to win four Olympics in a row. First in 1948 in the Firefly, then in the Finn in 1952, 1956 and 1960. Göran, who then sailed an L-dinghy, was extremely inspired by him, *"that you could sail both so fast and high was impressive."* (Paul reached the top mark without tacking, which every-

Göran's Finn with the name 'in the right place'

one else had to do.) Göran wanted to be as good as Paul one day and therefore started sailing the Finn.

Göran received many different tips from Gunnar and Sture, one of which was to get so close that you could read the name of the boat in front. Most Finns at this time had their name visible on the transom. It was a way to build self-confidence, not despair, but motivating, and maybe catching up. According to Göran, it was a very good 'measure' there was speed in the boat if you caught up, even if you were behind.

Early on Göran realised how important it was to have a good sail. In the 1950s sails were made from cotton, before the switch to Dacron. At an early stage in his career, he ordered a Dacron sail from Carlsen Sails in Denmark. When Göran tried it, there was a crease in the sail, but he was very fast anyway. He contacted them and complained. Göran was then told to send down the sail "*so we can fix it*", which Göran did not do. He was afraid that the sailmaker would copy it, as he thought it was very fast. It was very common during these years to try to steal ideas and take good initiatives from each other.

According to Göran, the friendship and helpfulness in Marstrand was very good when it came to getting different things fixed, regardless of whether it was table tennis, ice hockey and, not least, sailing. If Göran needed help with his rudder, he went to the 'workshop' (Marstrand's

Göran in Finn with sails from Carlsén sails in 1960

Mechanical Workshop), where they turned off the lathe and helped solve the problem.

Göran did not receive any major financial support from his parents for his sailing. However, it was obvious that help was given with towing of, say, 3-4 boats down to Långedrag. Göran trained in the Finn, back and forth towards the shoal at Kopparnaglarna. When there was a lot of wind, almost a storm, his father stood at the starting point at Strandverket and watched, so if he had capsized he would have received help. According to Göran, many Marstrand residents thought, "Is it necessary for the boy to be out sailing in this harsh weather?" Göran himself thought it was good and necessary to develop; of course there were a few broken masts, but for the most part, it was possible to repair them. Sometimes it became necessary to buy a new one and then his father had to show up with financial support.

The Andersson family also contributed in other ways. When the American champion and sailor Fred Miller visited Marstrand, in September 1961, he was invited to live at home with Göran's parents. Before the visit, in August, Fred had, as the first participating American, won the bronze medal in the Finn Gold Cup 1961 in Travemünde.

Fred lived with the family and got accommodation and food, but it was not entirely without problems. Plaice was served and Miller attacked the fish by dividing it into three equal parts without removing the bones. It did not go very well; he sat with his whole mouth full of bones. Before the meal the next day, Göran's mother Aina contacted a relative who had more experience of American eating habits. The tip she got was to buy meat in larger quantities and fry it. Miller looked happy when this was served, put everything aside and chewed with gusto. Others in the Andersson family, two adults and four children, had to make do with eating sauce and potatoes. According to Göran, he lacked *"all sense"* and his mother was not so happy about the visit.

The Finn, designed by Rickard Sarby for the 1952 Olympic Games in Finland

GÖRAN KEPT HIS Finn on a pontoon at Strandverket. It was made of oil drums, tires and used materials, which he got when they demolished a pavilion at Societetshuset. It was, according to Göran, *"the world's best boat park"*. Here you could launch and recover the Finn all by yourself.

Göran started sailing the Finn in 1955. His first boat was S59 and it was bought from Lasse Myrén in Gothenburg because it sailed so well. The dinghy was partially damaged on the fore and aft decks and had a broken tiller. The next Finn was an East German build, S127. These boats were very affordable at this time. The next Finn, S144, was built by Lennart Thörn in Karlstad in 1959. At the time all Finn sailors wanted boats that were made of mahogany and varnished. However, this boat (S144) was already painted and

Pontoon for easy launching and recovery of up Göran's dinghy

faired. When Göran realised, or was rather persuaded by Lennart, that a painted dinghy would be faster, the choice was not difficult. His brother Sture later bought this boat, which he sailed successfully for several years. Göran has had a number of Finn dinghies, including S304, manufactured by Elvstrøm, then S347 and then S449, which was built in Holland. This boat S449 I owned myself and sailed for a few years.

It was with Finn S144 that Göran's career in the class really began to take off. Based on old result lists from this time, we can note the following. At the Swedish Championship in Mariestad in 1959, Göran came fourth. The following year, 1960, in his old hometown of Lysekil, he came third. In 1961 at the Swedish Championship on Lake Mälaren, the club island Rastaholm, Göran won all five races, which is reproduced later in the text.

In 1961, Göran Andersson was 'Man of the Year' according to Till Rors magazine. Here, all important Finn races during the year and the results Göran achieved were reported. The following quotation suffices: *"Göran Andersson has been almost unbeaten this year and if he was to be named Race Sailor of the Year in Sweden, he would be difficult to ignore."* (Source Till Rors med segel och Motor nr 22, 1961, Bengt Hornevall.)

In 1963, he ordered a new Finn from Newport, and received S516. As an example of producing the best boat speed, Göran has a memory from this particular dinghy. The rudder vibrated when he sailed, so he tested it and replaced it with a Harken rudder and the result was that the boat became sharper. A number of Marstrand guys both built and sailed Finns, which created good friendship, joint training and useful competition.

Göran realised the importance of training correctly early on, partly by understanding how the skaters and skiers of the time practiced group training and partly by reading Paul Elvstrøm's book on sailing 'Sail to win', which could be called 'The Sailors' Bible'. When I asked Göran about this book, which I happen to know was published in 1967, he tells me that there was an earlier version in Danish: 'Joller og Kapseglingstaktik'. It was thus the early Danish version that Göran managed to borrow. There he remembers that Paul wrote, that it takes at least 10 years before you become a good and recognised sailor.

Göran's Finns have all been named Explorer. When asked why he used this name, the answer was that it was influenced by the United States, where during the 1950s several rockets were launched with the same name.

Finns S 516 and S 449 on the Marstrandsfjord

A prerequisite for sailing fast is that you have to have the 'right' mast. That is, to be able to tune it so that it fits the helmsman's weight and sail. In early dinghies, the masts were made of spruce. All L-dinghies had spruce masts, but for other dinghies it turned out that there were better alternatives. They began to use other woods, partly parana pine, a South American twig-free wood (Brazil) and sitka spruce from Canada. The spruce turned out to have excellent properties for masts for different dinghies.

Early in his career Göran got in touch with furniture carpenter, Gösta Larsson, living in Ytterby. They started collaborating in making masts, which is described in more detail in the section on Marinex. After a while, Anders Waern also came in as a mast maker.

Anders Waern was active in the traditional skating club IK Wega. Göran's contacts with Waern meant that Marstrand sailors could train in the winter with the skating club, mainly leg training at Ullevi. Organised training was at that time something new in sailing. Training was also conducted in Marstrand, mainly in the school gymnasium. A gym teacher and Magnus Löfgren assisted with this. On Saturdays, they did 'gymnastics' and played 'basketball'. They also had cardio training on the fortress hill with Kurt Lückner. Kurt was a very good canoeist from Marstrand.

Olympics in Rome 1960 and Mexico 1968

FOR THE 1960 Olympics in Rome, the Pentecost regatta at Rastaholm on Lake Mälaren, and the Swedish Championship in Mariestad were the basis for selection. Göran was appointed to represent Sweden in Finn and he went down to Italy with the Swedish pentathletes. He was on site for a whole month, first in Milan (where the team lived and trained) then together with the other sailors in the Olympic squad. The races themselves did not take place in Rome, but in Naples.

Before the sailing competition in 1960 the boats were drawn by lot. The boat Göran got was not good and it leaked when he launched it. He had to seal the hull himself as best he could. Several countries brought sparring boats with them to the Olympics, which could help them tune the boat and crew to achieve maximum speed. Some sailors had their own boats and masts to be able to train to the maximum. Other Nordic sailors from Norway, Denmark and Finland brought sparring partners with their own boats. Only Göran and the Japanese sailor, Yasuo Hozumi, did not have their own training partners, so Göran made a very good connection with him. Göran met Yasuo again in 1963 in Japan and spent the night (slept on the floor) at his home before the pre-Olympics.

Japan's national sailing team, including coaches and leaders, later visited Marstrand. The friendship has meant lifelong contacts and Yasuo has visited Göran several times both in Marstrand, Kungälv and most recently in 2012 in Ödsmål. Göran and his wife Ingrid have visited Yasuo in Japan.

Paul Elvstrøm was not only a very good sailor. He was also smart when it came to the equipment on the raffled Finn dinghies. He made sure to 'fix' the masts he considered did not bend correctly, and broke them before the races. This he did with three masts. He also made sure that the booms broke by using a lot of power when sheeting. The organisers got so tired of him that they finally let him decide for himself which mast and boom he wanted. Of course, Paul won the Olympics this time too. He was so superior that he didn't have to sail the final race.

Göran in his slow Finn finished in 28th place. According to the evaluation, which Göran sent to the Swedish Olympic Committee after the regatta, he writes: *"I was unlucky and got a bad dinghy, which both leaked and later became warped. It also couldn't be tuned properly as the boat was heavy in the bow."* The equipment and boats were very uneven, which is why Göran in the Swedish evaluation afterwards suggested drawing lots for each race, or alternatively allow sailors to use their own boats.

In the Olympic book from 1960, Thore is listed in the results, which is his second name.

For the Finn races at the 1968 Olympics in Acapulco, Mexico, it was Arne Åkesson from Gävle who represented Sweden. Arne finished in

From the Andersson photo album

seventh place in this regatta. The qualifying races were very hard, with several results used as the basis for selection. Göran seized the Swedish Championship title in Sandhamn, but after the last selection event in England, it was Arne who was chosen. More about these races and an odd disqualification of Göran at this regatta is described later in the book.

Göran was instead allowed to go along as a reserve, which also meant that Åkesson could train against him before the actual Olympic sailing took place. There were very troubled times in Mexico during this Olympics and Göran and some other sailors were accommodated in a monastery. When they knocked to enter, the door opened only five mm and it was probably a military guard who was holding on to the inside of the door. However, they were eventually let in and Göran remembers that just as they entered the monastery there was some wild firing outside.

There is more about this large event in the 1969 MSS yearbook, where Göran writes about the races as well as the following: *"During our time we got to participate in a lot of nice events, including bullfighting, life-threatening diving off a high mountain, big fishing with a 2.5 metre fish on the hook and some unforgettable evenings in exotic restaurants."* Somewhere in his extensive collections, Göran has a certificate that he has caught a *"so big fish"* (a sailfish). He remembers using herring as big as mackerel as bait.

There were several times that sailors were invited to a buffet together with representatives from various Swedish companies. He remembers a visit to a castle-like place on a hillside. There was a swimming pool at the bottom and a number of steps led to it. On each floor, at about 20 metre intervals down to the pool, musicians stood and played. When guys such as Pelle Pettersson and Sune Carlsson got to see the pool far down, they started rushing down the stairs at full speed and at least Pelle threw himself in with his clothes on. Göran said, "I was completely sober". In other words, both food and drink were amply served.

The sailing team also had time to visit the Graffman family, from Sweden, who lived in Mexico City. On this occasion, the Norwegian and Danish sailors were also invited. Holger Graffman was himself a sailor and for a time, 'banana king'.

For a number of summers in the 1950s, the Graffman family rented the villa on Backudden, where Göran Rutgersson now lives. Graffman's three sons sailed a J10 named 'Gittan', which was moored down on Rosenlund. Holger Graffman himself had a fantastic sailboat, the SK 95 'La Morena', which was sailed down from Danderyd every year. The boat was owned by the Graffman family from 1944 to 1978. (10.5 tons, length 20 m, mast height 23 m, built in 1922 in Berlin and it is still sailed today. See also the magazine Praktiskt Båtägande 2013.)

Races to remember

THE 1961 FINN Swedish Championship took place at Rastaholm on Lake Mälaren. As an example of good cohesion and nice sailing friends from Marstrand, Göran tells how it was then. He had a tent and a sleeping pad with him, not very good for sailing fast. Bertil Nicander, another Marstrand man, was, however, well equipped with a tent bed. When Göran won the first day's races, Bertil said: *"You can use my bed tonight and also in the future, if you win"*. Göran sailed well, which meant that he slept on the tent bed all week of the Swedish Championship and became Swedish champion. Winning all five races in this large fleet of about 80 boats shows how superior Göran was. Bertil fought well without a bed and placed 42nd. In this writing, Göran wants to thank Bertil Nicander and honour his memory when he unselfishly and voluntarily handed over his tent bed to a competitor. It was, for Göran, a big difference to sleep in it compared to his thin one lying on uneven ground. *"Thanks to Nicke, I won all the races in a big fleet."*

Getting support and assistance out on the water when racing is important. The Marstrand guys realised this early on. Bo Enarsson was present at the Swedish Championship sailing at Rasta. He remembers that he moved around in a small dinghy to support the sailors. Bosse remembers that Göran got an early start in the last race but that he won anyway. This is only to illustrate that Göran must have been in great shape during these races.

Before the qualifying races for the 1961 European Championship, it was very even between Boris Jacobsson and Göran. The Swedish Finn Association wanted the Ostsee-Regatta to be decisive for who would sail or stand as a reserve. During the trip to the races, Göran contracted a throat infection and had a fever of almost 40 degrees in the back seat of the car for two days. After medical treatment on arrival, however, he was able to start the next day. Göran immediately gained respect by winning the first race among 60 competitors. Göran was overall the best in these races, so Boris became the reserve. A few days later, the European Championship started in Warnemünde, where Göran finished second after a hard fight with Willy Kuhweide, who won. However, one can note in a quote from a newspaper report the following: "*Without a doubt, Göran was the most fit of them all down there and on every upwind leg he got closer to the lead.*" (Source: Article by Bengt Hornevall.)

Göran's memory of this regatta is that he had a big lead in the last race and Kuhweide was third. That should have been enough for Göran to win the championship. Second was then the Russian Alexander Chuchelov. He was from Tallinn, which then belonged to the USSR. When he was about 200 metres from the finish, Alexander's mast went through the bottom of his Finn and it began to take in water in the rough sea. This gave Kuhweide second place and so he took the overall win in European Championship.

The road to becoming a prominent Finn sailor

IT TOOK GÖRAN eight years to beat Paul Elvstrøm in his Finn S347 for the first time. He says that it was in Tokyo, Japan, at the pre-Olympic races in 1963 (before the Olympics, in 1964) that it happened. Göran was in the lead in the last race, on the last beat, and was ahead of Paul by 50-75 metres. Göran had already mentally prepared for what was to come and how the Dane would act. Elvstrøm began to tack on the slightest wind shift and showed that he could read the wind best. Göran had lost so many duels before against Paul. He would not fall into the same trap and take part in a tacking duel. Göran instead continued to sail without tacking or looking back; his focus was to look ahead and check which clouds gave the most wind.

After a while, Göran looked back at a wildly striking Paul, who was then about 150 metres behind. He 'just' had to continue with his winning and planned tactics. Göran knew that if Paul wanted to 'create a duel', then he was lost. No one could take the Dane in these situations. After the finish, Paul congratulated Göran. He really deserved it. After this description I asked Göran; "*Were you nervous?*" "*No, I had been beaten so many times before, but now I was mentally strong and had speed, not at all nervous.*" My own reflection after this description is that with a lot of training and experience, you eventually become so strong that you can beat even the best. From this trip, in addition to beating Paul, Göran remembers that he also bought several transistor radios and a TV for about SEK 590. He had the television set for several years.

GÖRAN ANDERSSON

World Championship in the Finn – Finn Gold Cup

THE WORLD CHAMPIONSHIP in the Finn class was sailed for the first time in 1956 and the competition was called the Finn Gold Cup. Göran took part a number of times, in several countries with outstanding results, but not as early as 1956. In one of these regattas, Göran did not perform very well despite the fact that he was in very good shape both competitively and mentally. It was 1968 and the event was sailed in Whitstable, England. It would also ultimately determine the selection for who was allowed to represent Sweden at the upcoming Olympics in Acapulco, Mexico.

At the start, in a race, Göran realised that it was an advantage to start at the port mark near the starting vessel. He also noted that the wind was shifting in his favour and that the current was with him. He prepared so that he was in good time (about 10-15 minutes) in the right position at the starting boat. The start went fantastically well and he was able to point well all the time so he reached the first mark without tacking and was thus very far ahead of all his competitors and he won this race by a long way. After the finish, it turned out that a number of sailors protested against Göran for an early start. There were hearings, but the

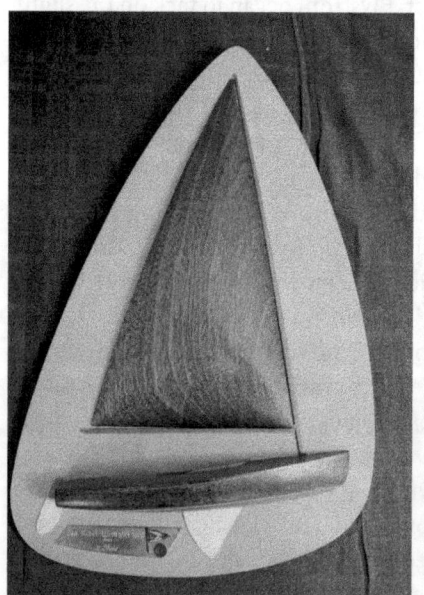 

Prize from Berlin, East Germany • There have been many medals over the years

jury rejected the protest about an early start. He had started so close to the starting vessel and no one on board thought he was over early. Despite this, the protest committee disqualified him for other reasons. It was considered that there must be something else wrong when Göran was so far ahead at the finish (probably the jury thought he had not rounded the first mark). Being a good sailor and being innocently punished for being able to read wind, current and sail fast, did not feel right. This disqualification naturally affected the entire series of races, which meant that Göran was not selected to represent Sweden in the Olympics in Mexico. He became a reserve instead. Overcoming such adversity requires a strong psyche, and not getting depressed, which Göran did not become. Instead, it was a matter of shaking off what happened and continuing to sail as well as possible. He also showed this at the tune up race for the Olympics in Acapulco, where he was allowed to participate as a reserve and sparring partner. He won this race in his own boat.

OK Dinghy

"*WHY DID YOU start sailing OK?*" This was my question to Göran at one of our meetings: "*I wanted to try the class, where there was a lot of competition, but mainly to become an even better Finn sailor. The OK Dinghy is very sensitive to different trimming, much lighter than the Finn. An example is how to sit in the boat; an incorrect position of only five centimetres means that the boat does not go as fast. In the Finn, which is heavier, you do not notice such errors as easily, but with different experiences from the OK Dinghy, I would probably sail faster in the Finn. My assumption was correct for the year 1968, where I won the Swedish Championship in Finn and also had several good results in other races.*"

The OK Dinghy was designed in 1957 in Denmark by Knud Olsen as a training boat for young people after the Optimist dinghy and before the transition to the larger Finn. The OK Dinghy quickly had a major international impact in several parts of the world.

Gunnar and Sture Lückner were also very important when it came to OK Dinghy sailing. They helped start the construction of some OK Dinghies in the fishing port in Marstrand from 1960-61. Four boats were built in the first round, and one of the builders was brother Sture Andersson, who built S9. These boats had masts from Skarven in Karlstad and Italian Salatasegel. The following year, more boats were built by Leif Enarsson and others. Additional OK Dinghies were built both in Societetssalongen (the big assembly hall from 1890) and on Koön (Uno Larsson's house). The OK Dinghy quickly became very popular. Between 1961 and 1964, about 1,200 OK Dinghies were built in Sweden, where Marstrand and Marinex strongly contributed to the explosive development.

OK Dinghy Sailing

GÖRAN THUS STARTED sailing the OK Dinghy in the 1960s. In 1965 he became Swedish champion in the Luleå Regatta, which was held at Rödkallen, a famous former pilot site.

He has also two World Championships in the class. The first world title was in 1965 in Great Britain, where they sailed at Hayling Island. There were 118 boats from 12 nations. Göran was not so well known in OK Dinghy circles at the time. Danish sailors who previously dominated the class were, according to their own statement, taken to the cleaners, as they quickly learnt how good Göran was.

Göran then got an opportunity to sail an OK Dinghy in Australia. He was invited to the First International Ocean Races, as the reigning Swedish Champion and world champion. The competition took place in October 1965, with a number of races on Australia's east coast with swaying palm trees, azure sea and white sandy beaches.

The Boomerang Prize

The gold trophies from the OK Dinghy World Championship

Transporting an OK Dinghy all the way to these races was not easy. A transatlantic ship carried Göran's boat to Adelaide, and the boat then proceeded to the city of Cairns in North Queensland on the Pacific coast. This transportation was extensive and cost a lot of money. Göran was not prepared to pay for all this himself, which is why the organiser booked a double-decker aircraft. In fact, the cigarette brand, Peter Stuyvesant, paid for the transport.

There were several long races, both out at sea and inside the harbour. Göran succeeded well and won a number of races including the Cairns to Green Island race. In the first race he won with a lead of five minutes. The last main race was from Green Island to Ellis Beach. The interest in this regatta was great. The races were filmed for TV from boat and helicopter and radio reports were going on all the time – just over four hours. The final sprint into the finish was witnessed by 16,000 people, with four sailors finishing within 15 seconds of each other, with Göran winning. There were 20 lifesavers who carried the dinghy with the winner, Göran, up on the beach. Next to it, the Swedish flag waved at the height of the palm tops. After the finish, Göran was crowned 'Coral Sea Queen' at the end of the International OK Dinghy Ocean Races. (Source: Göran's written report in OK-bladet 12/13 1965.)

GÖRAN ANDERSSON

1966 års innehavare av
Trafik-Bores gyllene ankare
mottager sitt pris av H.K.H.
Prins Bertil på utställningen
"Allt för sjön" den 8/3 1967

The Golden Anchor prize

The following year, 1966, the OK World Championship was held at Veerse Meer in Holland, where Göran won again. There were 88 boats from 10 countries. It should be noted that there were 13 Swedish boats among the first 18. The Swedes had completely succeeded in taking over the dominant role that the Danes had previously played.

The 1967 World Championship took place in Montreal Canada. Here another Marstrand boy, Björn Arnesson won while Göran took bronze. Erik Fromell from Sundsvall took the silver. "The Swedes put the whole world elite in their place." There was a lot of writing in the press about Björn beating his boss, as both worked at Marinex.

An exciting story can be told from 1966 after the World Championship in Holland ended. On this occasion, Göran also took a Finn and after the OK Dinghy Worlds, Göran went to the Finn Gold Cup in La Baule, on the west coast of France. So he now moved on with Finn sailing in focus. There was great crowd with 150 Finns from 26 countries. The Finn races did not go as well as in the OK Dinghy World Championship. Göran finished in 13th, but the best Swede. He says that it was very a difficult sailing area with a lot of tide. During these races, Göran brought Rolf Erneborn as a boat fixer and handyman. Göran says that

Rolf was the perfect handyman, could arrange everything from setting up tents (they were camping on a football field), maintaining the boat and not least cooking. Göran remembers that they did not go to a restaurant once during the regatta. Rolf Erneborn's view on this cooking is that he had found a local shop that sold good meat. *"It was just case of throwing the piece of meat into the frying pan."*

When the races were finished, it was time to head home, as always with tight time margins. There were ferry crossings, which were already pre-ordered. They drove home via Paris and drove past the Arc de Triomphe before further travel on the highway towards Belgium and Holland. When they came halfway to the first border crossing, Göran needed to pee. He stopped at a parking place and hurried out into a bush and attended to his needs. He jumped back into the car again and drove on. Rolf was in the back of the car, a station wagon, sleeping. They took turns driving and sleeping. When Göran, after a good while, began to approach the border and a customs station, he said: *"Rolf, get the passports."* No answer. Göran thought he was just heavily asleep and shouted much louder once more. Still no answer. Göran glanced back and found that there was no Rolf in the car. What to do? Turning the car around and starting to look for Rolf was not the easiest thing. When he had been driving for a long time, almost where they had stopped for the break, he saw Rolf come jogging towards him on the other side of the highway. Rolf was picked up and then it was not possible to turn around until the next roundabout and by then they were almost inside Paris again. Göran's comment about this event during our conversation was: *"We did not become enemies because of this and we had time for the ferry as well."*

Here, I also allowed myself to interview the other person in this story. Rolf described how he experienced the same situation. He remembers the journey home very well, not only because he was 'left astern' but also for some 'other events' during this journey. On the way down, one would cross the German border on the way south through customs. A zealous customs officer stated, after reviewing all documents, green card etc. that the papers (die Papiere) for the trailer were not in order. They were not allowed to cross the border. What to do? *"We must first get some food in our stomachs, then we will see how we can solve it all."* They found a tavern, ate a little and then Göran asked the staff if they had a typewriter. Well, after some hesitation, the staff found an old typewriter. Göran blew away thick layers of dust and then he put in the trailer papers and began to write in what was missing. Then it was off to the border, but another crossing point where they were allowed to pass: *"Alles in Ordnung"*. When I agree with Göran regarding this story, his brother Sture is present. Immediately they start talking about this opportunity at the French border. Then suddenly I understand that a similar situation happened once before. This second incident with border crossing is reproduced a little later.

The reason why the return journey went via Paris was that Göran wanted to show Rolf France's capital and sights. The agenda also included the purchase of perfume for Göran's then wife. When Göran tried to read out everything that was on the note for perfume purchases, the clerk was quick and grabbed it and picked up all the goods. "Stop, stop," said Göran. He probably only bought half of what was on the list, but Rolf remembers that it was expensive anyway.

They had time for some sightseeing as well, went up to the Eiffel Tower and from there they could look down on their car with trailer, boats and masts. Towards evening, they continued on the highway north, stopping at a large truck parking lot for the night in order to get much-needed sleep. In the car, a fairly large Fiat station wagon, they had two tent beds. In the morning, Göran was a little more alert than Rolf and went out to fulfil the needs of nature. Rolf also did so a little while later, and standing by the roadside, he suddenly saw the car drive away

Three dinghies with masts and other accessories could be transported with a Volvo Duett

and disappear. Strangely enough, *"I did not lose my temper, or get scared,"* said Rolf. However, he must have been quite affected because he does not remember what he was wearing. *"I think it was a little more than underwear, but I thought Göran must soon discover that I am not with him."* Rolf began to walk in the direction in which the car had disappeared. After a while, (quite a long time) he saw Göran driving on the opposite side of the highway. Rolf managed to get over and jump in. Göran then said that when he approached a tollbooth he said: *"Rolf, give me the wallet",* no answer and finally he discovered that Rolf was missing. Göran's comment on the situation that arose when Rolf got into the car, *"I thought you had passed out back there when I started back on the way."* Sometimes Göran can be 'really funny' in pressured situations, Rolf remembered. Unable to reverse immediately, they had to drive back to Paris to turn around. According to Rolf, the staff at the tollbooth (at the time, manual service) looked at them a little surprised when they passed for the second time, but without paying. It was a rather unique carriage they travelled with.

Marstrand Yacht Club (MSS)

ACCORDING TO GÖRAN, MSS has played a crucial role in supporting the sailors. Through various activities and financial support, opportunities were given to develop sailing and compete in larger competitions. Among other things, they had a lottery on the pier to raise money. Travel grants were given to Marstrand sailors to enable them to take part in competitions in another places: 'help for poor sailors'. This gave great opportunities to compete outside the village. People supporting this were Ewert Magnusson at the fortress, Bengt Ryding, Magnus Båysen, Jan Berglöw, Bertil Rönnberg (the owner of the company that made the drink FEST-Is) and not least Erik 'Kicken' Larsson, MSS's longtime chairman.

As early as 1960, 'Marstrand's Dinghy Club' was formed as a section within MSS and Göran became chairman. In 1965, a clubhouse committee was created within MSS with the task of raising money. MSS organised pop music concerts in Societetssalongen during the summer.

A further example of how MSS chose to support its sailors was that the club was also involved in health matters. It had been established that several sailors at various competitions abroad became ill, which reduced their ability to compete. Therefore, within MSS in

From left: Göran Andersson, Stig Gillborne (chairman of the Swedish OK Dinghy Association) Göran Dahlström, Clive Roberts, Björn Arnesson (world champion), Leif Enarsson, Guy Liljegren, Stig Boysen July 1967

1966, the idea was raised, through various measures, to prevent illness and to raise the state of health both physically and mentally. The programme for physical exercise, doctoral lectures on various issues such as hygiene, infectious diseases and eating and drinking habits in different parts of the world were intensified. Ahead of the 1967 OK Dinghy World Championship, where six of the 12 Swedish sailors were from Marstrand, MSS contacted the Swedish OK Dinghy Association with a proposal to link a doctor to the national sailing team before the World Championship. The request was then directed to county doctor Dr. Arnt Meyer-Lie, with whom MSS had already collaborated. He undertook the task as a sailing doctor for the entire team and carried out a number of measures before the trip, such as a complete medical examinations and necessary vaccinations. From various pharmaceutical companies and the Swedish Pharmaceutical Association, bandage equipment and first aid kits were received for all conceivable needs. These preparations and the on-site support in Canada allowed the sailors to perform at their best, both in terms of physical and mental condition with a health that could be assumed to be at an absolute peak.

The Swedes also brought with them an MSS mechanic, Ingvar Kristensson, who together with doctor assisted with support both on land and at sea (with a high-speed motorboat). During the half hour before the start, vitamin C in the form of oranges was distributed to all the Swedish sailors. In Canada, the press, radio and various TV companies paid attention to the Swedes' healthy lifestyle and the whole thing was the subject of several interviews. Very soon, 'the doctor of the Swedish team' became an institution, which was hired by over 80 sailors from 12 nations. (Source MSS Annual Report 1968.)

When I ask Göran about support from sailing doctors he completes the picture and says the following: *"We sailors from Sweden arrived at the World Championship in Montreal to be accommodated and live in a convent boarding school. Dr. Arnt Meyer-Lie did not approve of this accommodation due to vermin. The monastery had to be cleaned up first before we could move in."*

Swedish sailors took all three medals, gold to Björn Arnesson (MSS), silver to Erik Fromell, from Sundsvall, and bronze to Göran Andersson (MSS). From the results list, you can also see that there were five Marstrand boys among the first 15 boats, a result of both hard training and enormously good preparation at all levels.

Honorary gift, awards, letters and Christmas cards

GÖRAN RECEIVED A painting by Martin Werner Poser, a popular artist with a studio in Marstrand. He believes that it was in 1965 that a number of mainly Marstrand residents, 25 of them, gave him this nice gift in connection with Marstrand Day's races. The gift letter to Göran states the following text: *"With this gift of honour, the undersigned would like to show our great appreciation for your great interest and sacrificial work for sailing and sports education for the youth in Marstrand."*

That Göran is an honorary member of both MSS and the Marstrand Local Heritage Society may not need to be mentioned, but of course it is.

Göran has received a lot of cards and letters from his various opponents in sailing. He must have been an esteemed sailor that most people liked, at least on land. As an example, Göran shows a Christmas card from Alexander Tsutselov, an Estonian sailor who took silver in the Finn at the 1960 Olympics for Russia. The USA, Australia, New Zealand and not least Japan are also represented in the letter harvest. All these letters and cards are examples of the different friendships that Göran has established with sailors all over the world.

GÖRAN ANDERSSON

Göran with poster painting
Christmas greeting from the USSR

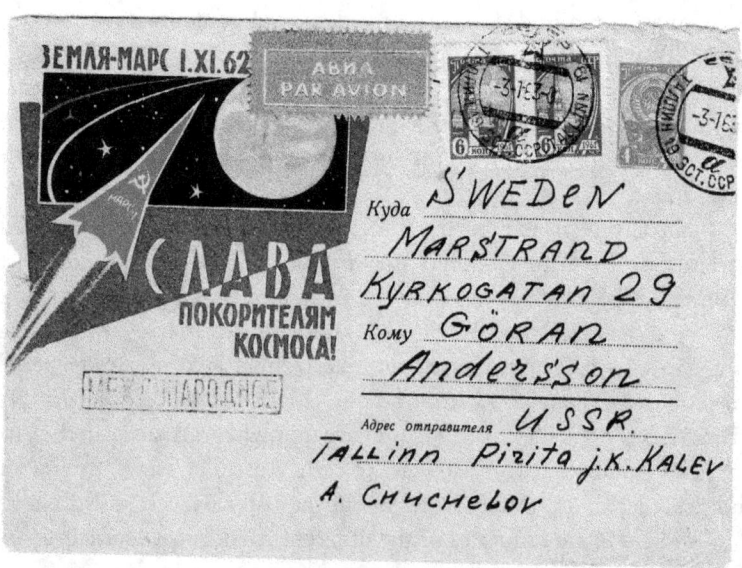

BJÖRN ÖRTENDAHL

The biggest thing that happened to Göran in the sailing world

THE AMERICA'S CUP can be seen as the start of organised racing and has been sailed since 1851. The first race was decided in England, where the schooner America won. After this first win, the trophy they competed for was named the America's Cup. The American sailors won over all challengers, mainly from England and Australia, for 132 years until 1983. Then the Australian boat Australia II won in Newport and defeated Dennis Conner from the USA. The skipper of Australia II was John Bertrand. Göran Andersson and Marinex played a great part in that victory.

The background to this story can be found on regatta.nu from 2011. The films contain both Pelle Petterson's conversation about John Bertrand and an interview with Göran about the correctness of Pelle's story. It's a film where another legend in sailing, Pelle Pettersson, tells a very interesting story about how good the Marstrand boys were and especially Göran Andersson. Here is a summary of what Pelle tells in the segment:

The meeting between John Bertrand and Pelle Pettersson took place in Portugal in 2011. John asked Pelle if he knew Göran, which Pelle of course did. John then asked Pelle to greet Göran and thank him for having succeeded in helping him achieve his lofty goals of becoming successful in sailing.

John sailed faster with his Finn after switching to Marinex sails and masts. Göran and Marinex delivered a mast, with the right bend measurements, and a Finn sail that suited his weight, all delivered on time. John was very impressed after testing the equipment. He therefore hid both of them. John did not want to show anyone else how fast he went with this equipment. The sails and masts were first used again at the Australian Championship, which were won by John. He also won the Olympic selection for the Olympics in Munich, where he placed fourth. At the next Olympics in 1976, Bertrand took bronze.

John's sailing success led him to becoming skipper of Australia II's challenge for the 1983 America's Cup. John Bertrand and crew, in the 12mR boat Australia II, managed to defeat the USA outside Newport, Rhode Island, and for the first time in 132 years take the trophy outside the USA. In part two of the film we hear how Göran listens and confirms how it happened.

According to Pelle, this story is worth preserving for posterity. He is certainly not alone in thinking so.

It was not only through Pelle's greeting that John Bertrand thanked Göran. On the one hand, Göran has previously received a letter of thanks and on the other, John once came, completely unannounced, to the sail loft in the City Hall in Marstrand to show his appreciation. In the interview with Göran, his accuracy in noting winds and currents from different races is mentioned. Göran also passed on his knowledge to other Marstrand sailors. I remember myself that before the 1963 OK Dinghy Swedish Championship, which took place in Marstrand, all of us Marstrand boys gathered in a school hall next to Göran's home. He presented an overview of various tactical details and currents. When I myself look in my notes from sailing at a young age, I find a paper (an A4 page), which we received regarding the currents. The document was addressed to MSS active sailors and was about the 'experts' tips' regarding the capriciousness of the Marstrandsfjord, which was certainly important, perhaps especially for Göran Dahlström, who won this championship. It was the first in a series of MSS successes in OK Dinghy sailing. I myself had bought an OK this year from Marinex and Göran, but I never had any good results. When I asked Göran at a meeting during the writing of this book, if he remembers this paper, I get instead a 15 minute description of the outline of all the points on the paper. It is a complement to Göran's excellent knowledge 55 years later. It shows how his advice has given other sailors possible success, especially point 7 on the old list, *"measuring the current with a fishing line with a sinker weight from a local sports shop"*. Now I get a regularly updated instruction. *"That was how we did it then, but now I have developed it all and when I give advice to others, it sounds like this. Instead of a fishing line with a sinker weight, use paper towels. It does not float on the surface or be affected by the wind but only shows the current. However, the paper may sink a little too fast. Then it is better to use an xxx.* (Göran does not want to reveal everything.) *What would it look like if all sailors did this out on the Marstrandsfjord,"* says Göran when we go through it all at a later time. *"xxx is built differently, which does a much better job. It does not sink as fast. Used correctly, this will be an excellent tool, and you have a much better picture over the direction of the current."* Experience has spoken, something he generously shares, though not fully. Anyone who wants to gain more knowledge about weather and currents can read Appendix II, where Göran himself has written and summarised a number of tips worth reading. *"A little insight into the head of a good sailor."*

Fantastic stories: a visit to the king of Thailand

ONE OF THE most famous people ever to sail an OK Dinghy was probably King Bhumibol of Thailand. It is no exaggeration to say that in Thailand he was considered a god, both during his lifetime and not least after his death in 2016.

His great interest in the OK Dinghy meant that he sought the support of a giant in the class, Göran Andersson and the Marinex company. The king built OK Dinghy TH27. When Göran was sailing in Australia, in 1965, he was invited by the king to come and give advice and tips. Göran flew from Perth in a plane that was so heavily loaded with military equipment that it could barely take off. When he arrived in Bangkok, a limousine was waiting and Göran was received 'royally' by Bhumibol. Someone who flew there at the same time, albeit in his own helicopter, was US President Lyndon B Johnson.

The King had a lake with several dinghies in the palace area. There was an Enterprise, a Snipe and an OK Dinghy. The latter was built and fitted out by the king himself. Göran had to help him with sails and mast rake and make sure that everything was 'ok'. The King was short in stature and also quite light, so Göran also helped explain how he would design the sidedecks, so that he could hang out in the best way. It apparently succeeded well, for the King later won the gold medal in the South-East Asian Games in Phuket in 1967. This day, December 16, 1967, has been the national sports day in Thailand since 1986.

Göran's visit ended with the King's wife Sirikit inviting him to lunch, as the King was to meet the President of the United States. Bhumibol must have received a lot of inspiration from Göran as he had a total of four different OK Dinghies during his active sailing years. One of them was sailed by his daughter Ubol Ratana. She was noticed in February 2019 by the press and media when she briefly ran for the post of Prime Minister.

This story could have ended then, but here comes an incredible epilogue to this adventure of King Bhumibol. At the beginning of 2018, Stefan Sjöström from Marstrand was on a cruise to Hong Kong and Thailand. Among other things, he sailed 5o5 with Göran and was for a time employed at Marinex. What does he discover, but a great monument and tribute to King Bhumibol? On the large monument there is a picture of the King sailing. Here you can clearly see the Marinex mark in the sail; also the mast and boom are from Sweden. This is how a country

GÖRAN ANDERSSON

King Bhumibol used Marinex sails and rigs

pays tribute to its beloved sailing king. Below is Stefan's story about how he got to see the monument and then photographed it.

Stefan Sjöström's story about how he discovered and took the picture:

"In 1973, I was asked if I wanted to sail the 5o5 World Championship in Hong Kong with Göran Andersson. It was easy to answer yes, and we went there with great excitement, not least when our respective wives could travel with us. Göran was the crew and I was a helmsman. We finished 15th among about 85 dinghies, and the best Nordic boat. In February 2018, my wife and I were with my brother and sister-in-law on a cruise to Singapore and Hong Kong, as well as Thailand. It was really exciting to see Hong Kong again after so many years and after all the political changes that have taken place there. The cruise ship was relatively large and sometimes anchored quite far from the main attractions, which we passengers could visit. The shipping company had arranged and booked these trips.

During the visit to Thailand, we made our own excursion to one of the most important tourist destinations, Pattaya. We walked on the main street along the beach (actually a terrible environment). My brother and I stopped at a bar and had a beer, while our wives looked in different shops. As we sat there, I saw a large picture of King Bhumibol across the street. I knew from time immemorial that he sailed the OK Dinghy and that Göran had been to Thailand and met him. We thought it seemed very interesting and stumbled across the street. There was a very well kept monument, with a marble base and a perfect picture of the King with a Marinex mark on the sail. I immediately took out my cell phone and took pictures. When my sister-in-law came, she also took pictures with a real camera. My first thought after the photo shoot was that this must be shown to Göran, which we also did."

When we finished with the picture of Bhumibol, Stefan started recalling some sailing memories and we return to the fantastic sailing adventure in Hong Kong in 1973. He continues to tell about the host championship. *"When we got there, we were accommodated on Hong Kong Island with different families. Göran lived with Christian von Sydow, who worked for the Ekman trading company. He was also an avid sailor and sailed a lot in the waters off Hong Kong. Christian had at some point sailed across the border into China and remained there for 1-2 months. At this time, Hong Kong was an English possession, so the Chinese guarded the border closely. Göran also had the privilege of using his private driver for various trips."*

"My wife and I lived with a Frenchman, who was the head of the Bank de Paris National in Hong Kong. We could take advantage of our host's private driver. The bank manager was a very strange man, completely crazy about sport. When he was at home, three TV sets were on at the same time where he watched various competitions, dog racing, horse racing and motor racing, all to be able to play at these different events. At one point, the Frenchman had a party with invited jockeys where lots of cognac was drunk. It should be noted that at this time Hong Kong was the largest consumer of cognac per capita and the finest you could drink was this particular brown drink."

Stefan also remembers a dinner for all the sailors, which was strange. The participants had been out and done 2-3 races during the day and were invited to dinner at a top Chinese restaurant. They were placed at different tables, 12 at each (2 men in each boat x 85 = 170 sailors). *"We were tired and hungry but mostly thirsty after a hard day at sea. Several asked for something to drink, the staff nodded and came in with whole bottles of fine cognac. No sailor dared or wanted to drink this without asking for something else, preferably alcohol free. The staff nodded again but they just brought in more cognac. After a while, several gave up getting something sensible to drink. They started taking cognac slowly. Göran, who did not drink alcohol, laughed a lot at his friends who slowly started to get a little drunk."*

Another memory that has stuck with Stefan is an episode, right at the start of a race at this World Championship. *"What is it?"* Göran shouts and points to something that comes floating. It was a dead cow, not exactly what you want to meet on a starting line.

"Already at this time, in 1973, they were technically well advanced. All starts were filmed and afterwards you could see what it looked like, always the same mid line sag. In terms of sailing, it went pretty well for us. We finished 15th boat and were thus the best Nordic participants. In addition to the races, we also had the opportunity to pay a visit by train to the Chinese border.

When we came ashore in 1973, we pulled the boats up on the beach. It was a very rural area. When I now returned there in 2018, there was nothing left of the beach. There was now a large recreation area with hotels and large buildings. When we sailed there in 1973, there were a number of junks, but in 2018, not a single one."

More events that must not be forgotten
The border crossing to France

STURE ANDERSSON SAYS: This happened in 1962 during a trip to Bordeaux. We travelled in a Volkswagen beetle with two Finns behind on the trailer. It wasn't a short trip, just over 2,000 kilometres. At the border between Belgium and France, there was border control. At this time, there were strict border controls, partly due to the war of independence in Algeria. The French underground organisation OAS tried to prevent Algeria from gaining independence through various terrorist methods. This meant that at the border controls there were armed guards with machine guns. Göran and Sture were already stressed on arrival after being delayed two days when they were forced to repair their car in Germany due to an engine problem.

At the border control, the Andersson brothers quickly established that the customs spoke nothing but French, which neither of them did, thus there was no chance at all to be able to communicate with them. Their passports and green card (for the car) were checked ok, but for the trailer, there was a sign-off missing in the document. They were not allowed to pass border; they felt hopeless. They thought they could drive on anyway, but then an armed guard suddenly stood in front of the car with a drawn weapon. They could not drive on, just turn around and go back to the nearest town. There they managed to find a Belgian motor organisation and with their help, filled in the missing information. Then they proceeded to the border control, though obviously not the same one that refused them entry into France. They crossed here without any problems. On the way down, they spent the night in Paris, where Göran had a Finn friend.

The stay in France and journey home from Bordeaux

ONCE IN FRANCE, they sailed on a lake at Lacanau, which lay close to the coast, Sture remembers. They stayed at a beach hotel (closed during the winter) and ate their meals there. When the waiters asked what they wanted to drink with the food, they both answered "milk". The service was extremely surprised they didn't drink wine, which was strange. As none of them drank alcohol, this choice was natural, but not for the French, who began to hate them. When the races were over, they received a very large bottle of alcohol as a farewell gift from the hotel. Although none of them knew the contents, they took it with them. Sture just remembers it was some type of alcohol. They were really uneducated on this subject.

When they arrived in Denmark, they visited Paul Elvstrøm to pick up a Finn, which they would take home for training. When they arrived in Helsingborg, neither of them were very comfortable with clearing the Finn through customs

The brothers came up with a solution. They drove into the red customs lane instead of the green one and then went to the customs with the big liquor bottle. "We have won this liquor bottle as a prize and we would like to take the bottle home, even if we do not drink alcohol." Customs did not know how to act. They called more colleagues, were puzzled and studied the regulations, and consulted with each other. What could the value of the bottle be? All the customs were impressed with the prize. If the boys had won the bottle, they will not pay any duty for a sailing prize. Go home and have a good time. That they 'happened' to forget to tell about the extra Finn, which they picked up from Paul Elvstrøm, is probably out of date today. Sture remembers that they later turned the bottle into a lamp with a nice shade.

It was probably not the first time that it happened that you 'forgot' to clear various things. The need for a well-functioning sewing machine, a second-hand Pfaff, meant that it was included in a Finn from West Berlin in 1963. The city was at this time one of the densest areas of boats in Europe and was far ahead in terms of dinghy sailing. It also had good sewing machines to make sails.

GÖRAN ANDERSSON

Snus delivery

IN 1968, BERTIL Rönnberg was a deputy on the MSS board and a summer resident at Instön. Bertil was also team leader in the Swedish Hockey Association. Professionally, he was a manager in the company that sold the drink FEST-iS, and which actively supported the Marstrand sailors and MSS. (FEST-iS was launched in 1961, and was Sweden's first still drink without carbonation. It was packed in a 19 cl large pyramid package and cost 33 öre each at the launch.)

Göran Andersson and Gunnar Åsblom, both talented Finn sailors, were invited to Ski-Yachting in Cannes. The invitation also included their wives. Bertil Rönnberg must have known this when he contacted Göran. *"The Swedish national ice hockey team will participate in the Winter Olympics in Grenoble, but we have a problem. The ice hockey stuff has arrived, but the snus and the FEST-iS have been stopped by customs – can you help us?"* Immediately they loaded Göran's Finn full of snus and several packages of FEST-iS (the snus would be enough for several weeks for a number of players and leaders) and on top they put Gunnar's Finn and then took it from Sweden to the Olympic village in France. The journey went well and they just had to leave the cargo inside the Olympic area in Grenoble and then go on to Cannes. There was no alpine downhill skiing. *"On the west coast we had no habit of this sport. We just sailed."* Despite Göran's snus delivery, the Swedish national hockey team only managed fourth place.

Göran on training with sailors double booked for a wedding

EXACT TRANSCRIPT FROM GYC (Gothenburg Yacht Club), 100th anniversary publication 2017

Göran Andersson:

Finn training session - a grey cold Saturday 14 May 1977 - Marstrandsfjorden - northerly wind 7-8 m/s.
12-15 participants including Guy Liljegren, Kent Carlsson, Magnus Liljedahl, Gösta Ericsson, chairman of the Finn Dinghy association.
Escort boat - MSS Skäreleja with Erik 'Kicken' Larsson, MSS chairman.

We gather north of Sillesund, west of Klöverön at 9 o'clock.

Rabbit start to the finish line at the Skäreleja islet. The downwind was free all the way to Sillesund, where it was a new start.

After the first finish, Magnus asks me – *"Göran what time is it?"* and I answer *"Nearly 10"*.
After the second finish, Magnus sails up to me again and wonders *"Now what time is it?"*
Nearly 11. *"Why do you keep asking about the time? What is the matter with you?"*
After a while, Magnus answers - *"I'm getting married today."* *"When?"* *"3 o'clock"* *"Where?"* *"In Hagen's Chapel."* *"Come on, there's plenty of time."*
A poised Magnus then says that they are going to the photographer first and then I shout when he sails away. Come again tomorrow, same time and place. Then Magnus raises his right arm in the air.

Round 3 has started, good conditions, Guy and Kent at the top.
So Guy sails up to me – *"What time is it?"* *"A quarter past 12."* *"What's up with you now?"* *"Gittan and I will be at the wedding."* *"Then there is plenty of time, we sail another lap, come on."*
Guy is then disappointed and explains that, *"We should be part of the photography and then, we will be a witness."*
Round 4 was an easy match for Kent C.

EVERY YEAR, THE Gothenburg Yacht Club awards the Yachtsman of the Year award. In 1966, Göran Andersson received the association's first award. The standard is constantly rising and a large number of well-known and talented sailors have been awarded for outstanding results at the Olympics, World Championships and other famous races. The current trophy has therefore had to be extended so that all name plaques can fit.

Göran stopped racing Finn in the 1970s but as can be seen from the above article (GYC) he was still sailing the Finn in May 1977. According to Göran, he was then mostly involved in training other dinghy sailors and helping to further develop young people in sailing. Göran chose other challenges, which meant that he started sailing at sea. In 1977, he won overall at the Skaw Race, on the small course, with his 'Accent' (quarter tonner). The following year, he was a sail trimmer on the winning boat, 'Big Mouth' (half tonner), on the main course. The boat not only won the Skaw Race on the main course but also overall, which in

Muskeviken

sailing language is called Tota. Skaw Race was at this time a large race with upwards of 200 boats and the west coast equivalent to the Gotland Runt.

Sailing with Pehr G Gyllenhammar
(President of Volvo from 1971-1990)

DURING A FIVE-YEAR period, Göran sailed a lot with Pehr Gyllenhammar, both in a Nordic Folkboat and IF boat. He was also crewing when the Gotland Runt was sailed in 1975 in Pehr's Maxi 95, 'Amanda'. I have read a logbook, written by one of the guests, which the crew received after sailing. The author describes the writing as ironic, but I also perceive it as quite humorous and the writer is affable with everyone on board. I feel that what the author writes about Göran is quite angled and ironic but funny nonetheless. Here are some great excerpts:

GÖRAN IS PRESENTED as follows:
  The first mate is Göran, he is responsible for the masts and sails on board. He does the same in civilian life. Göran is a master crew, never really happy with the sails, but a connoisseur in his art. He is cheap to run - lives mostly on soft drinks and sandwiches and is happy to leave nobler goods to others. His nickname will probably be 'Loranga' or John Blund (John Blund is a nickname for a sleepy person in Sweden). He is

extremely happy to take a horizontal position.

A little later in the logbook, the day before the start, the following is noted about Göran at a lunch:

'Loranga' - listen and be amazed - has taken a beer with the food and Skipper has had time to demonstrate the vacuum cleaner.

For once, 'Loranga' does not sleep. Instead, it looks like he is lying and looking at the sky from the foredeck. In fact, he is watching the big spinnaker and plays artfully with the guys. In fact, he succeeds quite well.

There was no top result for 'Amanda'. The crew did not manage to interpret the wind and current well enough, despite Göran's solid work with the sails.

Driving both in Sweden and abroad

ON ONE OCCASION in connection with our meetings and conversations, I went with Göran in his car. *"You have driven a large number of miles on the roads during your long career, right?"* "Yes, you can believe it. *Work until 16-17, then into the car (with dinghy on trailer) and drive to Stockholm for a race the next day at 10 o'clock. I was once stopped by a police officer for speeding. I do not have time for this,"* said Göran. *"I will go to Stockholm and sail tomorrow morning."* "I've stopped bigger stars than you," the policeman said. When I ask Göran how high a fine he received, he answers the following: *"No, I was allowed to go on and I did not receive any fines."* Performing at the top after long working days and many miles behind the wheel showed Göran's ability to perform well in various competitions.

Books inspired by Göran's sailing successes

THE AUTHOR LARS Hesslind from Gothenburg spent a lot of time in Marstrand and ran a writing school there for several years. On one occasion many years ago, probably sometime in the late 1960s, Lars was sitting at Berg's café on the quay. According to Göran, he then saw the following. Göran was out with a small boat when he saw a 'seagull' trying to catch a small eider cub. Göran quickly went to save the little duck, and managed to hit the gull with an oar and at the same time save the eider cub. He rowed away to Malepert with it, where a flock of eider mothers lay with their young. He let down the eider cub, which quickly entered the herd. Some time after this, Lars Hesslind interviewed Göran, about both the episode and sailing. They quickly made good contact. Lars had a son who went to Göran's sailing school.

During the first half of the 1970s, Lars wrote a number of books that took place in Marstrand and which were largely about sailing and also about Göran and the Marinex sailing school, including 'Balloon in Top', 'Last Minute' and 'Stiff Gale'. Later, in 1980, Swedish television filmed a TV series in seven episodes based on the books. Göran was asked to be part of this series but he refused.

Here is a short excerpt from the second book in the series entitled 'The Last Minute' (an adventure book in a racing environment).

"Göran Andersson was Marstrand's most famous sailor. He had brought home several world, European and Swedish championships in different boat classes to Marstrand. He had made Marstrand a respected and well-known name in sailing circles around the world. The people of Marstrand were very proud of their Göran. He had even been elected to the municipal council just before Marstrand became part of Kungälv municipality. Of course, he was the idol for all Marstrand's sailing youth."

PART 3

ENTREPRENEUR

THE MARINEX COMPANY

"GÖRAN, HOW DID you come up with the name and brand Marinex?" This was my question at one of the meetings. This is what Göran said: "My dad, Thore, had a Snipe named Marine and I had a Finn named Explorer. We sat down and talked. Dad's boat name and my Finn name were tossed back and forth. We chose Marinex as the company name, the first part of dad's boat name without e and the first two letters on my Finn dinghy. It became Marinex."

The contacts, experiences and networks that Göran gained through his work with West Coast Boats meant that in order to continue and expand the business, he started his own business. The Västkustbåtar company was wound up due to illness. It was 1959 and the company name became Marinex. At this time he was only 20 years old. This meant selling various boats, starting sailmaking, and initiating mast production. However, Göran had previously made some preparations, made contacts and visited a sailmaker in Gothenburg, Hasses Segel, to learn and gain the necessary knowledge.

From both old letters and advertisements it appears that Marinex was transformed into a limited company in 1961. The name then became MARINEX - Göran Andersson AB.

It was not enough to 'just' create the name Marinex, but it was also important to develop a visual brand. How did it happen? *"I sat and sketched over various fast-paced situations with a sailing dinghy, though not so complicated. It came quite naturally."* From the beginning, the mark consisted only of the sailing dinghy, but it was a bit time consuming to sew it to the sail. *"We later modified the symbol and Håkan Erneborn developed it to be used with self-adhesive textile prints. It was much easier and faster to get hold of, and more efficient production."*

Kits for Optimists

GÖRAN STARTED SELLING Optimists in kits. He received an order from the City of Gothenburg for 100 kits. He even had to deliver sails for these dinghies. The sails were first sewn by Magnus and Sonja Båysen at Brömsegårdsviken, on Klöverön. The kits were made by Fredrik Johansson. After a while, they plotted and cut sails in Arne Johansson's basement. Sails were also sewn at home in Fredrik Johansson's basement. Fredrik Johansson's wife, Anna, and their neighbour Ester Schultz took care of this work.

From this time, Göran's younger sister Margareta remembers sitting in the basement with Fredrik and Anna making sailing cloth samples. These were small pieces of cloth in different colours, which she cut with pinking sheers with serrated blades, so that the samples were serrated at the edge. She then bundled a number of different colours for mailing

Company logo

It was Marinex sails that mattered

to different customers and stakeholders. Margareta got 2 öre (2 cents) each. It was quite quick to do this, so despite the modest payment, she remembers that it could be a decent daily allowance for a youth.

Göran himself never sailed the Optimist but made sure that the class was well established in Sweden. Marinex manufactured and sold kits more or less by mail order. He did everything to support and develop the youth activities, partly by being a role model himself, and partly by developing sailing for young people. A big driving force was of course to sell sails and masts. A typical action for a true entrepreneur.

Mast production for dinghies

HAVING A GOOD mast for your dinghy was important. Göran realised this early on, not least at the Olympics in Rome in 1960 where he experienced how Paul Elvstrøm was able to win. "*Paul and most of the participants brought their own masts.*" However, not Sweden, with Göran as a representative of the country. When Paul sailed with a number of raffled masts, he understood that their own masts they had brought from Denmark were of much better quality. Of course, it was much easier for Paul as a three-time Olympic champion to get through his requirements. Therefore, he made sure to use them in the Olympic sailing. Yes, he won this time too.

Gösta Bohlin was a mast manufacturer for dinghies in Kristinehamn. He also made masts for Dragons and sailing canoes. In 1958, Göran saw an advertisement for the carpenter, Gösta Larsson, best known for decorating clothing stores. He lived on Granstigen in Ytterby, "*good street name for a carpenter*". Göran started collaborating with him and placed an order for 10 masts. These were made in Ytterby from spruce. The material was bought from Utländskt Trä, a company located in Gothenburg on Marieholm. As a small and newly started company, it was important for Göran and Marinex to handle business relationships in the best way. Göran therefore joined the West Swedish Shipyard Association, (a network of shipyards and boat builders on the west coast). This gave him longer credit with Utländskt Trä. It took a long time until the masts were finished for sale and income was made. He could also receive good advice from other boat builders and shipyards

A temporary 'painting department'

who had experience of both working with spruce and who had traded with the company in question before.

Göran says that Utländskt Trä stored logs of spruce (approx. 70-100 cm in diameter) in large basins in Göta Älv. They also had a system of hoses that sprayed water from above on the part of the log that was above the water surface. All this was done so that the logs would not crack, before they were taken up for sale and further processing.

After the company had sawn the logs into planks (approx. 3 x 6 inches), they were delivered to Ytterby and later Marstrand. These planks constituted the raw materials for masts, two halves were milled out, partly to save weight and partly to build up the mast in the right way. They were then glued together and planed to the right elasticity and shape. The end product then became a very well functioning mast. The mast and sail were adapted to the sail's length and weigh – a tuned combination.

To increase the production of masts, Göran later bought a small property on Marstrandsön. This was behind the hot bathhouse and was sold by Jean Dahlström. It was a former barrack, which was used in the construction of Hotel Marstrand. The price was 5,000 kronor. The purchase also included certain tools, such as a combi machine with an associated steel mill, which came in handy for milling out mast blanks.

In this workshop, Anders Wärn, who was 10 years older than Göran, began to build up the business. Wärn was not so stress-resistant so the collaboration did not work fully. Both the Erneborn brothers worked for a time with mast manufacturing, first Rolf who had to complete some production, when Wärn left and later also Håkan.

Leif Josefsson then became 'the good carpenter' and after a while the mast expert, and took over the production. He developed the manufacture of masts, first in wood then in light metal. The business was later run independently of Marinex under the name L J Marstrands Spars. Leif then bought the property from Marinex. In 1978, Leif built a new larger factory on Koön and became a neighbour of Marinex.

During a period in the 1970s, Nicander also produced masts for both Finns and Trissjolle (a Swedish double handed boat that still has championships today). Göran sold the masts for the Trissjolle to the ABC factory in Kungälv. (ABC was the manufacturer of Trissjollar.)

Göran remembers this production with pleasure. One of his biggest competitors and comrades during the Finn era was Boris Jacobsson from Uppsala. He was a very good sailor, European Champion in 1962 and 1963, Finn Gold Cup silver in 1962, four Swedish Championship wins and was the Swedish representative in the Olympics in the Finn in Japan in 1964. When Boris trained and sailed in Marstrand, he lived with his wife Tina at the Nicander family home. Rolf, who usually built and repaired houses, now also started making Finn masts for Marinex. According to Göran, it seemed that Rolf liked this. He really got involved and made sure that the masts went well. Rolf always had a smile on his face when he talked with the sailors. Rolf himself successfully sailed a J22 Långedragsjulle.

Marinex Sailing School

MARINEX SAILING SCHOOL had up to 1,000 students for about 10 years. Among the students were several children of well-known business leaders with a Marstrand connection. Göran mentions the children of Pehr G Gyllenhammar, Peter Hjörne and Ingemar Johansson (Mossholmens Marina) as examples. Some of the manufactured Optimist kits went to Sigtuna, where our current King sailed one of these. In Sigtuna, director Winquist at Stockholm's Enskilda bank also had children. They sailed and went to the same school, which provided opportunities for Göran to sell both boats and sails. The parents' association at the school provided a lot of these sales successes, according to Göran. Several of the parents were connected to Marstrand and a number worked in the Wallenberg corporate sphere with connections to both the business and sailing world, which benefited the development of Marinex.

The sailing school used, among other places, the Corvette property (via collaboration between GKSS and MSS). With the help of local forces (carpenters Ingvar Kristensson and Holger Steen, electrician Erik 'Kicken' Larsson and plumber Lennart Nilsson) it became a 'clubhouse' with a sauna. Göran proudly stated that everyone who did 'all the work' could use it for free. The sailing school was taken over in 1973 by MSS, which MSS has continued to operate ever since.

Sail production and sail lofts

THE SUCCESS OF selling and manufacturing sails, as well as customer demand, meant Marinex was forced to expand production as well as rationalise and concentrate sail production. In the beginning, sails were manufactured in various basements, as previously mentioned, for exam-

Students and instructors at Marinex sailing school

ple, with Fredrik and Anna Johansson. As demand increased, the loft began to move around a number of times.

The first sail loft was in a basement in an apartment building, Bohusgatan on Koön (often called HSB). Mary Erneborn and Ester Schultz and others sewed sails. Göran's mother Aina worked with cutting reinforcements. Demand increased and it became necessary to have even larger and better-adapted premises.

In the early 1960s, they moved over to Marstrandsön. There, the choice fell on the former Stenström store, which became the next stop. The premises were rebuilt to better suit the business. Here the sewing machines were set into the floor. Jean Dahlström was responsible for the rebuilding. Now they could work more efficiently and rationally. The former Svalander coffee shop was, for a time, Marinex's office. After a while, Göran moved the office into the premises of the sailmaker and became a neighbour of Magnus Löfgren.

When the company moved its operations in 1963, Göran was in Japan training for the upcoming Olympics in 1964. According to Rolf Erneborn, he remained in the former Stenström's premises at least until 1967.

One of the boys who worked for Göran was Björn Arnesson. When he went to do military service, Göran had to find a replacement. He then sent a letter in October 1964 to Håkan Erneborn, who himself was finishing his term of military service. When Håkan was demobbed he got a job at Marinex, to become a sailmaker instead of building masts. Håkan still has the letter, which he showed me. Both Erneborn brothers eventually became very skilled sailmakers.

GÖRAN ANDERSSON

Town hall is the next stop for sail loft

THE NEXT STOP, when they needed even larger premises, was to move into the old City Hall. The town hall is Bohuslän's oldest stone house and formerly Marstrand's City Hotel. The reason for the move was Göran's protracted problem with buying a plot to build on and not being able to find any other suitable real estate.

On the ground floor of the former City Hall, small sails were sewn and on the second floor, up in the Crystal Hall, larger sails. In the former bar on the second floor, an extra floor was built and up there Mary Erneborn and Thora Dahlström sat and sewed. It was Jean Dahlström who fixed the rebuilding. He had previously built the 'pit' with good results when they were in the former Stenström premises. Göran had his office at the top of City Hall.

Marinex had a customs warehouse on the City Hall's porch, from which canvas and materials could be picked up if necessary, after customs clearance. At this time there was a customs station in Marstrand in Sjömanshuset by the quay. In photos from the time in the City Hall and the Crystal Hall, you can see the templates laid out on the floor and that the sails are attached with awnings directly on the oak parquet. There were

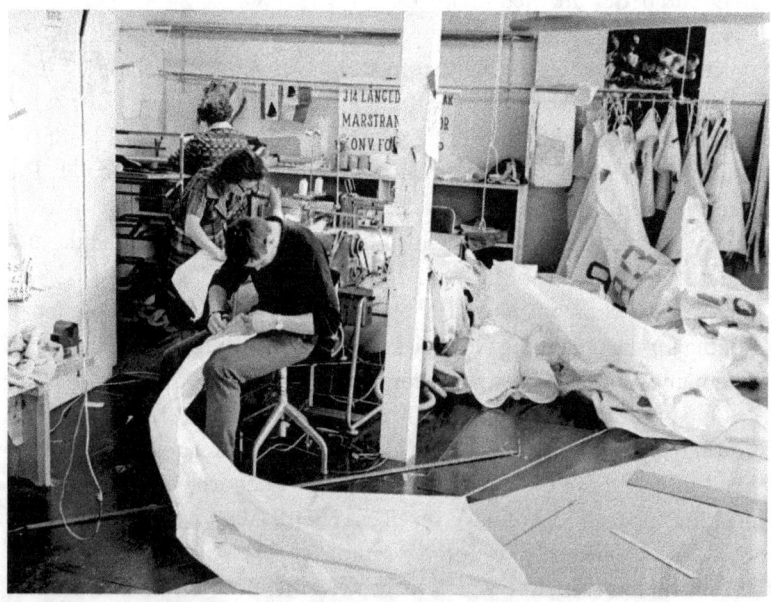

Sail making at the former Stenström store on Långgatan

no restrictions on how to use the room, but after the move, some parts of the parquet were replaced. It was mainly in the corners of the room that the new floor was most needed. At this time, the house was not K-marked (protected). According to Göran, these premises lasted for about 7-8 years.

Several young Marstrand boys and girls started their professional careers by working at Marinex. Many of those who chose to study further got a chance for a summer job with Göran. These included Stefan Nilsson, Anders Ryding and Kerstin Johansson. His brother Sture also worked for Göran and Marinex during the summer.

Marinex

Göran and Marinex expanded their operations on Korsgatan, Koön, from 1970, by selling boat and leisure items via the Marinex Yacht Shop. Göran's then wife Louise also worked at Marinex handling many administrative tasks.

New construction on Koön

GÖRAN FIRST ASKED the City of Marstrand and, later on, the municipal merger Kungälv municipality about a plot to build on. Transporting everything to and from the sail loft was time consuming and very labour intensive. Sometimes this meant that you had to arrange transport yourself instead of taking the goods by ferry. An investment on Koön would therefore mean a significant improvement in many ways. Of course, the requirement was also to get a more efficient and functional room, although the Town Hall was quite OK. Göran therefore searched for land in several different places.

Sail manufacturing in what is today the Crystal Hall

An establishment on Koön in Åkerblom's property with a boathouse was perfect at a cost of SEK 150,000. However, the bank in Kungälv thought it was too expensive and therefore Göran was not given the opportunity to borrow the necessary funds for this purchase.

However, decisive for Göran to finally get the opportunity to buy a plot on Koön, where the old Arvidsvik bathhouse was located, was that he received an offer to establish his business in Rönnäng, on Tjörn (the big island to the north of Marstrand).

Göran had struggled for 7-8 years to get a plot to build on. First with the city of Marstrand and then after the amalgamation of municipalities, in 1971, with Kungälv municipality. From articles that Göran saved, as well as a few I read, it is clear how disappointed and frustrated he was over all the different trips. All correspondence with committees, administrations and boards of appeal, included seven full binders, according to an article in GP (Göteborgs Posten, the largest daily newspaper on the Swedish west coast). A lot of administrative hassle prevented a successful expansion of Marinex to develop and meet the customers' great demand for sails. Göran now says in retrospect that everything was a problem, from the angle of the roof to the colour of the tiles on the new building. It was also discussed about what billboards he was allowed to put up on the house.

Finally, when Marstrand / Kungälvs municipality realised it was a real risk that Marinex would move from the municipality, they made it possible by offering a new building area to keep Marinex in Marstrand.

Marinex was, for a period of time, Marstrand's third largest workplace. If Marinex were to move to Tjörn, this would mean a large loss of tax revenue for Marstrand / Kungälvs municipality. Marinex employed several women and also a large number of younger men. There would then be a risk that the younger people would choose to move to Tjörn and settle there. Relocation would also largely mean unemployment for the women who certainly would not want to travel to Rönnäng by road. The sea route is not long but the Marstrandsfjord is not so nice for much of the year.

Before the construction of the sail loft on Koön, Göran asked his sailing friend Stefan Sjöström if he wanted to work with him and handle all negotiations with the municipality and procurements. Stefan agreed and also worked for a while in the loft in Kristallsalen before construction started. In my interview with Stefan about the World Championship in Hong Kong, we also get into the construction of the Marinex House on Koön. Stefan remembers a meeting with the city architect from Kungälv. The municipality considered that there was not enough good land to build on, 'only old landfill'. Marinex solved this problem in the best way, again an example of Göran's ability to find solutions to problems, but here with significant help from Stefan.

Göran had a customer, I think it was a Scampi sailor (a Scampi was a half ton boat that was produced in the 1970s and was successful in Scandinavia), Stefan said. This customer worked at the then Skanska as a basic expert in the construction of single-family homes. In response to the objections from the municipality, Marinex replied, with the help of the expert: *"It is not a problem. We build the house on six building plinths.*

The Marinex house on Koön was completed in 1975

Production was streamlined in appropriate premises

Then it will be good and no problems." The municipality agreed to this solution and the house is still stable today. Håkan Erneborn designed the interior of the sail loft, with submerged pits for the sewing machines. Stefan was also responsible for the administration in the sailing shop, which was already established on Koön in the property where Göran and his family lived.

The new loft contained two floors, the upper floor of 275 m2 where sails were both designed and cut. Sail sewing occurred on both floors. Upstairs, it was mainly larger sails that were sewn together. They designed a form of gutter, called half-pipe located diagonally to the sewing machine, where the taped yarns lay. This made it faster and much easier for the skilled seamstresses to join the stiff fabric together.

During one year, Marinex consumed approximately 40,000 to 50,000 yards (37,000 - 46,000 metres) of sail cloth. Ninety percent of the fabric used was manufactured by Bainbridge in the USA.

One of the oldest and largest sailmaking companies on the west coast was Syversen Segelmakeri on Smögen (established as early as 1888). Marinex collaborated with them for several years, mainly in the manufacture of larger sails for cruisers, such as for instance the Vindö 50, 75 and 90, among others. The deliveries thus mainly concerned new standard sails for the large boatyards, which during the great boat boom of the 1970s required large and extensive sail lofts.

Stefan Sjöström also remembers that Marinex – before Rutgerson Marin was established – distributed rings for sails, which were manufactured by Göran Rutgersson. Göran Rutgersson's father, Östen, sat at home and packed the rings, which Marinex then distributed around the world. My question to Göran after Stefan Sjöström told this story was: *"Did you get any commission?"* The answer Göran gave: *"It was 0 kroner."*

MANUFACTURE OF OPTIMISTS AND OK DINGHIES

FREDRIK JOHANSSON AND the company Plywoodbåtar started manufacturing kits for Optimists and then also OK Dinghies in the former Knaving's metal foundry on Koön. The property, which was small from the beginning, was gradually expanded, as the business grew and the demand for various dinghies increased. Göran Dahlström started there, and later, also Rolf Erneborn. The OK Dinghies that Fredrik manufactured and that Marinex sold were at this time the world's most successful. They won the World Championship in 1965, 1966, 1967, 1969, 1970 and 1972. In total, the production amounted to about 400 dinghies. (Source: Completely OK, Robert Deaves.)

DEVELOPMENT OF SAIL PRODUCTION AND OF PRODUCTS FOR SAILORS, THE INVENTION OF A NEW MARINE CLEAT

GÖRAN REALISED EARLY on how important it was to make the production of sails efficient and at the same time maintain high quality. An example of this was when Göran and Rolf Erneborn went to Kumla to buy used machines for sailmaking. The United Shoe Machinery Corporation (USMC) produced various industrial machines for the shoe industry. Marinex bought a hydraulic punch for the production of figures and reinforcement pieces. Three 'knee joint presses' were also purchased for pipe riveting of headboards and for pressing small eyelets into Optimist sails. These machines made sailmaking more efficient. Marinex produced

Fredrik Johansson

about 1,000 Optimist sails in each year, so a time saving of a number of minutes per sail therefore meant an enormous amount when it came to efficient production, while also maintaining high quality.

Another important factor in the production of sails is the quality of the sailcloth used. Here Göran was the first and only in Sweden to get a machine for tensile testing of sailcloth. The manufacture of sailcloth, just like other textile production, involves weaving together two perpendicular thread systems (warp and weft) into a functional and strong canvas. Through the purchase of this machine (Istron Tester), Marinex was now able to tensile test the purchased sailcloth both on the diagonal 45° and perpendicular 90°. It was now possible for Marinex to investigate that the sailcloth obtained was of the right and promised quality. Of course, this was a quality control that enabled better and more durable sails. The machine was so advanced that it had a printer, which drew the elongation in both directions on a diagram.

Marinex applied for a grant via the county administrative board to be able to buy it. They received 50 per cent in support (about SEK 30,000), which was gratifying. The machine's advanced functions meant that Chalmers University of Technology visited Marinex on various occasions to use it for its own tensile tests as part of its research work.

There was the lack of a good fitting to attach trimming ropes to various dinghies, both home-made and others in the marine industry. There was a fitting on the market, a pipe jam cleat, which were manufactured partly in Sweden (Gnosjö and Karlstad) and partly in England. However, the functionality was not very good; the ropes would slip far too easily. Fredrik Johansson and Göran figured out a better solution. Fredrik bent a piece of metal as the first prototype. There, the rope got stuck properly (they used a starter cord for an outboard engine as a test). Göran had previously had contact with the Järnförädling, which had operations in Flen and Västervik. They made products such as anchors and good quality tools. Working together, the cleat was developed in stainless steel, and Järnförädling sold it throughout Sweden and in Europe. It was a sales success even though it was quickly copied. Göran and Fredrik received a commission of 10 Swedish öre each for each cleat sold.

The dinghies that were built also needed a good stainless steel bracket. This was manufactured by Werner Bengtsson at Instön, according to the provided instructions, and it was important that the fitting was easy to grip during launching and recovery, and was strong enough to hold when towing. It was not uncommon for about 10 dinghies to

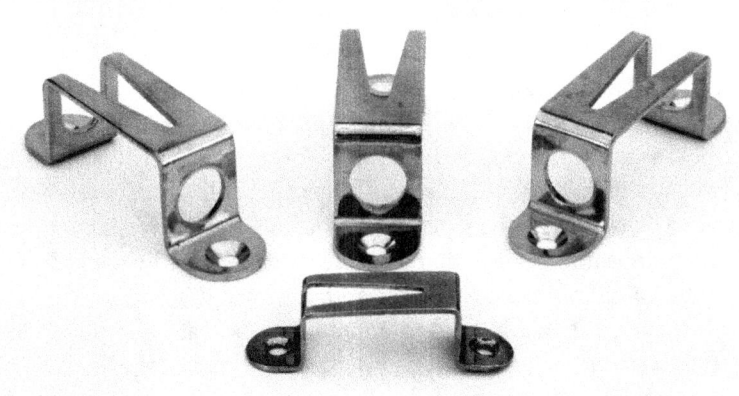

The Marinex cleat was much appreciated (and copied)

hang in a long row after an escort boat when towing out or in. Werner Bengtsson also designed rudder fittings and locking cleats for halyards. These were manufactured by EVO foundry in Gnosjö. Some exports also took place to England of EVO's other products. Göran remembers that Marinex sold their boat hooks in packs of 200 pieces.

Products for boat manufacturers and sailors

THE ABC FACTORIES in Kungälv and Ytterby were for a time a major producer of sailboats, all with the brand name Triss such as Lill-Triss, Triss-Jollen and Stor-Triss. The company was initially best known as a manufacturer of sports equipment such as skates, skis, tents and bags. When it entered the marine industry, it began collaborating with Göran. ABC marketed the 'Sailor' life jacket, battens and sailing shoes all designed by the world champion, Göran Andersson. He took a commission on what was sold, though according to Göran, these were small sums, but a welcome addition. Masts were also made, in sitka spruce, for Trissjollen through Göran's care. He says that at that time it was difficult to get good battens. Later he partnered with Svängsta in Blekinge (ABU, Abu Garcia), a manufacturer that was prominent in the production of fishing reels and spinning rods and other fishing tackle. This meant that ABU could also produce high quality battens.

Göran's used the knowledge gained from his long experience of sailing and racing on several occasions during the Marinex period. Influences and experiences from other sailors, especially from Marstrand, were used extensively. It should be noted that Göran, through Marinex, was one of the first in the industry to professionally combine mast manufacturing with sewing sails. It was a winning concept.

Another example of taking part in other people's experiences is given by Göran in the following way: The Star World Championship was sailed in Marstrand in 1970. The famous sailor and sailmaker Lowell North came to Göran and asked if he could come into the loft and adjust a sail, which he was not happy with. Of course, said Göran, who naturally followed with interest what North did with the sail.

It turned out that he moved and adjusted a seam one millimetre. Getting a perfect sail required knowledge and experience, which North had, a lesson that Göran applied in the future, when he changed his sails so that they would be better. This useful experience was also used to adjust and plan the masts to the correct bend. The sails that were tested together with these different masts could thus be sold with great success. They were thoroughly tested for each sailor depending on how much they weighed and how tall they were.

Together with many complementary and mutual business companies, such as Fredrik Johansson with plywood boats and Leif Josefsson with mast production, Rasmussen's production of canopies and mast socks and stainless steel production at Werner Bengtsson, on Instön, meant that Marinex was probably Marstrand's third largest workplace during this period, after the Marstrand shipyard and the pilotage service.

In 1977 there was a lot to do, which meant that Göran outsourced the sewing of sails to Samhall in Lysekil. In the past, he had sometimes outsourced this production to Marstrand residents. Both men and women sat at home sew-

Sailor life jacket tag

ing. These contract workers also cut panels and made different letters and numbers.

Sailmaking is a very personnel-intensive activity. The extensive operation now required both proper management and the right organisation to meet quality requirements and productivity, and to have satisfied customers. Göran demonstrated for a large number of years that he was able to successfully lead and develop the company in the right direction. He had no deep education in economics and leadership to rely on but he still succeeded. You can call this talent a 'business nose', an ability to succeed in business. At the same time, Göran emphasizes that everyone who was employed or involved in Marinex's production and sales was or became extremely skilled in their respective areas. According to Göran, both employees and partners were very accommodating and showed up on weekends when needed. That the business worked well was probably very much

Above: The sailbags still work. Björn Örtendahl and Göran
Below: Margit Andreasson

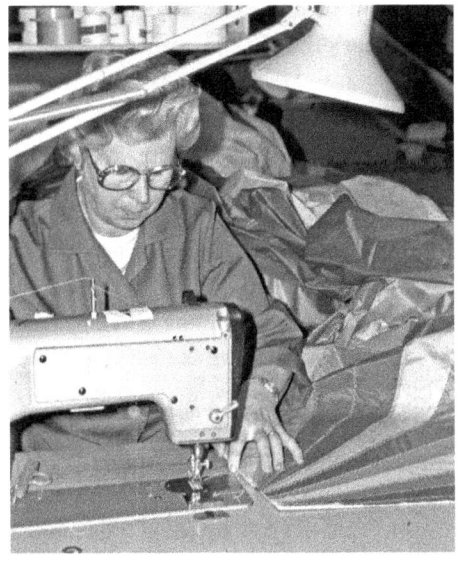

The Cementa ferry converted into a test rig

due to Göran's own behaviour and his prudence, something he modestly does not emphasize at any of our meetings.

Marinexsegel became a well-known brand. The company manufactured sails with 'the right quality', which gave buyers and sailors great success on the race course. Several of the boatyards in Bohuslän, which made quality boats, now equipped these boats with sails from Marinex. These included boatyards such as Vindö and IW. The manufacture of larger sails became more important, such as for offshore sailing. The distribution between racing sails and sails to the different sailboat manufacturers was about 50:50.

To ensure that the sails manufactured and sold were 100 per cent top quality, Marinex had several different land-based test rigs throughout the years. After the move to Koön, the company had a smaller land-based test rig and a larger float. The float was a former ferry, which in an earlier period was in service on Lake Mälaren and then for a time served as a Marstrand ferry to transport passengers. It was built of concrete and was popularly called 'Cementa' by the people of Marstrand. Now it was given a new function, lying outside the sail loft as a floating test bench. Sails could now be tested at the right height above the water surface.

Marketing and advertising

THROUGH GÖRAN, I have been able to access a selection of advertising material that Marinex used for advertising and marketing. Binders with a lot of data show how consistently and professionally they worked with these issues. Here, also, Göran made sure to use different contacts, experts both in Sweden and abroad to promote the company in the best way. There are several examples of advertisements in newspapers and various club magazines, sales and letters to both old and new customers.

An advertisement in the MSS yearbook from 1969 contains an advertisement from Marinex (page 35). In this advert you can see the fantastic results that were achieved with sails from Marinex.

When they joined Horizon in 1977 (described later), they invested in a large multicoloured folder of six pages. The images in this publication were self-produced, with Rolf Erneborn now not only working as a sailmaker, but also as a photographer.

Göran started an early collaboration with Volvo in several different areas. As an example, there is this picture.

Göran says that during various visits, such as to the USA, he always had to dispose of Volvo cars. Perhaps this is not so strange, as Göran for several years both sold sails to and sailed with Volvo CEO Pehr G Gyllenhammar.

Marinex established in Australia and New Zealand

GÖRAN TOOK ADVANTAGE of previous contacts and networks to establish Marinex on the other side of the globe, specifically in New Zealand and Australia.

At the Olympic Games in Naples in 1960, Göran became acquainted with Ralph Roberts, who sailed the Flying Dutchman (FD) for New

An early 'influencer'

Zealand. Ralph was at this time world champion in the FD after winning in Kiel. A few years later in 1963, at the pre-Olympics in Tokyo, Göran also met his brother Clive Roberts. He was both a Finn and OK Dinghy sailor and one of the best from New Zealand. *"The next meeting,"* says Göran, *"was in Brisbane when I was on my way to sail in Cairns. There I also met Clive's wife Beverly."*

Göran defeated Clive at two important regattas in Cairns in 1965. Despite that, or maybe because of this, they talked a lot about sailing and that Clive would eventually become an agent for Marinex. They finally agreed that Clive would come to Marinex in Marstrand to learn and participate in the production of OK Dinghy sails.

Clive became an agent and started sewing sails at home in his basement in New Zealand. Björn Arnesson travelled there and helped with the setup to make OK Dinghy sails, which now bore the Marinex sail mark. There were holes in the floor just like in Sweden for the sewing machine. Clive became an even better sailor and won several major regattas both in New Zealand and in Australia. He also became OK Dinghy World Champion in 1973.

Taking advantage of the seasonal difference between Sweden and mainly Australia and New Zealand was a concept that could be used. The sails and masts tested on the Marstrandsfjord during the Swedish summer could be sent to the other side of the globe, tested and ready for their summer season. This approach was used when Marinex was more established as a supplier. This combination (mast and sail) won two World Championships (1966-67) in Europe and one World Championship (1970) in the southern hemisphere. The box construction with a frame inside was taken from the manufacture of large masts for ocean-going sailing boats. It was a construction method that Göran became aware of through his collaboration with boat builders in the West Swedish Shipyard Association.

Unfortunately, Clive died very tragically in a car accident in 1975, leaving behind a wife and two sons. Rolf Erneborn was there a few years after Clive's death to help, so that another sailmaker could continue production in New Zealand.

As a sailmaker, Marinex also had an agent in Australia, William 'Bill' Bell in Melbourne. He was a skilled dinghy sailor and Australian champion in the OK Dinghy. It was Bill who received the order for mast and sail from John Bertrand in 1971 (delivery time 10 months) as previously reported. According to Göran, Bill was a 'big player' internationally in cinema and TV. He had the rights to broadcast the World Cup in Australia. The broadcasts from the Australian Open tennis championships were also handled by his company. The company had 50 trucks with equipment for arranging various sporting events. When Marinex inaugurated its new loft on Koön, Bill Bell was invited and participated. The following year he visited Marstrand again and sailed in Göran's Finn. At the beginning of 1979, Göran's son Gustaf had the opportunity to go to Australia, and lived with Bill and also went to school there for a term.

ONE OF SWEDEN'S LEADING SAILMAKERS

MARINEX CONTINUED TO develop the sailmaking business during the 1970s and in the autumn of 1977 the company became a representative of the American sailmaker, Horizon Sails in Stamford that they began after Göran had been over in the USA. Horizon's backbone in sailmaking was a unique computer programme.

"Göran, describe how it happened," I asked. *"The sailcloth manufacturer Bainbridge (founded in 1917), asked me when I was visiting the United States if I knew of computerised sailmaking programmes. We had probably heard something about it but not much more.*

I was then referred to Professor Jerome Milgram at MIT (Massachusetts Institute of Technology) in Cambridge, near Boston. Already in the

Staff at Marinex

mid-1960s he was a pioneer in computer-aided design of sails. I was very welcome to visit him and get acquainted with what he developed.

We got in good contact and then everything happened very quickly," says Göran.

This meant that Marinex and Göran were allowed to represent Horizon Sails of Annapolis, USA, in Sweden. There were two lofts in Sweden, Marinex and one on the east coast, which began to sew these sails.

Jerome Milgram is an extremely well known name in the marine and sailing world, mainly because of his way of testing the properties of sailboats on a computer, as well as changing and testing sails to get the 'right design and curve'. Göran had the opportunity to see his wind tunnels and other things he was doing for the development of sails. Göran told me that he also worked for NASA on other projects.

In my internet research on Milgram, it appears that during his 50 years career he has made countless contributions to marine architecture in areas such as theoretical hydromechanics, education, yacht design, and environmental protection (12 patents in oil spill technologies). He also led eight America's Cup design teams with great success.

He was really a big name and an expert, which Göran apparently got in good contact with, so that it became Marinex / Horizon in Marstrand. An advertisement from this time describes that Horizon had 'The world's most developed computer programme for sailmaking'.

Göran and his employees, Håkan Erneborn and Björn Arneson, were in early contact with other major international sailmakers to enter into various forms of cooperation. They visited Hood Sailmakers and Christopher Bouzaid in Marblehead USA.

Marinex began a partnership with Horizon

This meeting did not pay off on this occasion, as Hood in England had exclusive rights for the whole of Europe. A while later, in 1978, the company sent a letter to Marinex and Göran. It stated that the circumstances to represent the brand had now changed and that Hood was very interested and wanted to meet representatives on their next visit to the United States to establish cooperation. According to Göran, however, there was no new visit.

A CUSTOMER WHO SAILED LONGER THAN MOST

IN THE 1970S, Göran and Marinex got a customer who sailed very far and long with Marinex sails. It was Sven Lundin (now Yrvind) with the small boat 'Bris'. Sven built his first 'Bris' at home in his mother Kerstin's house in Långedrag in 1971-72. Then from 1973 to 1976, he sailed out into the world from the little island of Brännö. Marinex and Göran received a postcard from Rio de Janeiro, where Sven arrived from Las Palmas after 48 days. Sven has always tried to get everything as cheap as possible for his boats and this also applied to the sails. The fabric for Sven's sails was provided by Heathcoat Fabrics UK. Marinex never got paid for sewing them up. However, when he came home again, Sven gave a lecture for everyone at Marinex as a thank you for the help. Göran remembers that he brought a globe with him, which was always the easiest thing possible for Sven. It was an inflatable thing as big as a beach ball, drawn like a globe on which he pointed out and showed how he had sailed. Marinex's customers also got to listen to Sven's funny lectures.

GÖRAN ANDERSSON

Travel to the USA, shopping and holidays

DURING THE TIME Göran ran Marinex, he made several trips to the USA to purchase items such as sailcloth. Sometimes he travelled alone and sometimes together with different employees. One of these trips in the early 1970s became quite famous for several reasons. Thora Dahlström and Mary Erneborn had worked for many years sewing different sails. They started in the early 1960s and according to Göran, both were always available to do some work, working if needed both late in the evening and at weekends. When something needed to be done such as broken sails, repairs, alterations or extra fast deliveries, it was always resolved. So, Göran took these ladies on a 14-day trip to the USA, partly as a thank you for everything they did for him, and partly for their knowledge of sewing machines.

The purchase of specially equipped machines in New York was on the agenda. The trip first went by car to Oslo and Fornebu Airport, then flights with a stopover in Iceland. When they got on board the plane and into the air, a great lunch was served with Icelandic specialties. Everyone on the plane was very happy. Suddenly a choir, named Orphei Drängar, with its leader Eric Ericson, started singing (after he had hit the tuning fork against his head). The choir entertained the crew with singing as a thank you for the good food. *"There we sat in the middle of 'this wonderful gang',"* says Göran. *"It was a big surprise that we had the finest choir in the Nordics on board the plane. We were curious about what the choir would do in the US and it turned out that they were going to the East Coast and then to Florida to perform."*

"The plane landed in Reykjavik for a break, and at that time the airline paid for our stay on the island. There were different visits; we looked at hot springs with baths. Warm clothes were also purchased. The choir took part in this sightseeing. The journey continued to New York, and the choir entertained us with more singing as a thank you for the food and the pilots were praised for their way of handling the plane."

"We landed at JFK (John F Kennedy International Airport). Every now and then, Thora and Mary got to experience what it meant to be in a queue. We were over 400 people queuing for passport control and visas. The acoustics were good in the room so even there the choir sang, which was dedicated to customs staff and others. Ericson brought out his tuning fork again to make it sound good. Everything went well at the airport and then we went to the hotel."

The next day it was time for work, a visit to the factory for sewing machines and equipment. There were various used and renovated machines as well as new equipment for sale. The purchases of renovated sewing machines were well thought out and planned. At the 5o5 World Championship in Hong Kong in 1973, where Göran sailed together with Stefan Sjöström, they had had time to visit various sailmakers. Göran then took the opportunity to conduct 'industrial espionage', check the type and manufacturer of which machines were used – information that could now be used.

Göran, Mary Erneborn and Thora Dahlström on a trip to the USA

Then it was time for an excursion and sightseeing for the ladies. Göran would meet the top people in the sail industry, so how to make the ladies manage on their own? Göran came up with advice and also solved this situation. They each were given a matchbox and on it was the address of their hotel. Then it was just a matter of fixing a taxi and then they set off, only showing the box, when it was time to get back to the hotel. They also had time for a fantastic visit to Niagara Falls.

After New York, the trip continued with flights to Boston, where they would visit Bainbridge, a large international sailcloth manufacturer and accessory supplier of, among other things, test machines. The visit included a meal at a great restaurant; there was a warm welcome for them all.

Göran made large purchases of sailcloth, enough to last half a year. The sailcloth had to be laid up in a customs warehouse in Gothenburg at Packhusplatsen. As previously mentioned, the trip lasted 14 days, so there were many more experiences for the ladies, such as a trip to Miami. However, they did not meet the choir on this occasion but instead had time to visit Key West and look at both crocodiles and beautiful flowers.

The trip was an incredible experience for all of them, where Göran was not a manager but a 'friend' on the same level. The ladies did not know the language but with Göran as interpreter, everything was resolved throughout the trip.

Much later in 2015, Göran and his wife met parts of the Orphei Drängar choir. It was at a 90th anniversary celebration of a good friend of the family in Ljungskile. They were unaware that the choir would be there, the visitors were let into different entrances and then they ended up in the same queue.

After a while, it dawned on Göran that some of the people in the queue were from Orphei Drängar, the same choir that was on the trip to the United States all those years ago. When Göran asked if they remembered the trip, he got the answer, that of course they knew about the trip but that they themselves were unfortunately not allowed to join, which several of them were very sorry about.

Cake on Fridays

SEVERAL PEOPLE I spoke to about Marinex have wondered if I'd heard the story of the 'cake' on Fridays. Göran has not mentioned anything about this, which is why I raised the issue. It was like this, says Göran: "When we delivered sails, we told the buyer that when you win with these sails, you can come back and offer a cake from Berg's patisserie. At Bergs they knew that I liked princess cake so there were a number of them. One time I think it did not turn green but red instead. It must have been a bit of joke about which kind of cake I preferred."

Sale of Marinex

UNDER GÖRAN'S LEADERSHIP, Marinex sold its sails to about 100 different countries. About 200 championships were won with Marinex products. It developed into a successful company from Marstrand that really placed itself on the world map in terms of sail manufacturing. He was partly an elite sailor at a high level, which required extensive training, and partly a business leader. Göran says that when sailing in a Finn, a few years into his career, they started to have team leaders, something that was not so common in the beginning. It was good, but he remembers one occasion, when he called home to take care of Marinex and then he got the following comment. Bengt Hornevall, former Finn sailor and now leader, said: *"You are here to sail, you have to run the company later."* Göran was both owner and business leader with responsibility for a large sailing loft as well as a family breadwinner and father. One wonders how he managed to lead such a big business. In 1972, however, he had to slow down when it came to sailing at the highest level. Göran then had so much to do with the company and the approaching OK Dinghy World Championship in Marstrand, that he withdrew from the competitions in Finn before the Olympics in Kiel.

In 1979, Göran sold Marinex to ACAB - Marin, an agency for Baltic Boats. After a while, Göran felt that the work was not taken completely seriously. There were irregularities and the bank was worried. Göran then chose to quit Marinex. Some years later, in 1982, the company went bankrupt and thus a major player in the marine industry disappeared.

Göran's continued professional life

AFTER MARINEX'S BANKRUPTCY, Göran first worked as a salesman at Nordic Yachting in Henån and then he started at Asperö Handel. He worked there for many years, until 2001, selling sailcloth and other boat accessories.

Many heroes behind Göran's results

GÖRAN HAS ON several occasions mentioned a large number of people, who according to him were an important part of his sailing successes and how Marinex developed. If all these names were included, it would be a very long list. It must be a collective thank you to everyone, no one forgotten. *"A big thank you to you all for fantastic efforts."* However, we make an exception where Göran specifically mentions one of them, Erik (Kicken) Larsson, as one of the most important MSS leaders. He did everything including laying the marks and checking if anyone needed help on the water, which created great security for all MSS sailors, and not least for Göran.

Final words

AFTER ALL MY meetings and pleasant moments with Göran and his wife Ingrid, I have tried to reflect. Have I been too positive in what I have written, impressed by everything Göran told me about concerning his sailing and business life? Have I been blinded by a star? No, I have seldom met a more modest and humble person. He always emphasizes others, and that it *"went so easily"*. On the other hand, it emerges, without Göran pointing it out, how determined and visionary he has strived to be in his complex sailing and business life, often without the aim of great financial gain. There was a big difference from his sailing where it was always about winning. In addition, all the different documents and photos that I have had the opportunity to see, show how popular and 'fair' Göran has always been.

Every time I visited Göran, a new memory or story has emerged, which in most cases has been recorded and included in this book. Here comes the last one, which Göran himself wrote down for me. It is about when he, together with the boatmen in Marstrand and mainly the Säve helicopter division, saved 19 sailors from the storm in 1969. Unlike all of Göran's sailing adventures, this is an effort that saved 19 lives. Below is also a description of good seamanship in which Göran was involved, but mostly as a witness and not least as a photographer.

BJÖRN ÖRTENDAHL

The sinking of the vessel 'Agro Mayor', 22 September 1969, west of the small island of Hamneskär

GÖRAN WRITES: I was on Marstrand's quay at Björks Möbelaffär (a furniture store) equipped with my mini camera, a Minox (100 mm long, 32 mm wide and 17 mm thick). I was wearing rain gear and a sailing vest in the storm and was out to photograph the damage that the storm was causing.

Then two boatmen, Jens Kristiansson and Magnus Löfgren, came running along the quay and down towards the pilot boats. Magnus shouted at me; I was the only person on the whole quay. *"There has been a major shipwreck with a cargo boat. Can you help?"* I jumped on board with Magnus without even thinking, 'my life could be in danger'. The engines in the pilot boats had to be run hot and first the wooden pilot boat left the quay and then the iron pilot boat with myself and Magnus on board. There was a steady westerly wind of about 43 m/s. The captain of the cargo boat had contacted the pilot lookout because they needed a pilot, Magnus said. The pilot lookout replied that there were no vacant pilots at the moment. The captain was therefore advised to change course to the west and face the strong wind.

Magnus further says that after a while you could hear on the radio traffic the crew shouting: *"The engine cannot turn the ship and steer west."* The communication was silent and from the pilot lookout you could see the wreck when the ship grounded on the little island.

This was what Magnus with Göran on board and Jens in the other pilot boat knew, when they went out into the storm to save lives. Magnus and Jens were very skilled at handling the pilot boats in the hurricane and they slowly approached the wreckage of 'Agro Mayor', which now stood high on the Grösslingen skerry, just west of Hamneskär.

At this disaster, we were the first to reach the wreck. It probably gave the crew (about 20 people, we did not know then) hope of rescue. For us in the pilot boats, it was unfortunately frustrating to state, *"Rescue with a pilot boat is completely impossible".*

Suddenly, a moment later, a vertol helicopter (a specific type of rescue helicopter in Sweden) appeared, the 'Banana' from Säve helicopter division. The hope for the crew rose again aboard the cargo ship. Two rescuers were wired down from the helicopter to the wrecked ship and crew members began to be hoisted up. When 4-5 people were rescued, the helicopter flew up to the Carlsten fortress, the northern fortress

GÖRAN ANDERSSON

Agro Mayor sank in the 1969 storm
Agro Mayor

embankment, and offloaded the shipwrecked crew. These trips continued a number of times with firefighters and female soldiers taking care of those who had been dropped off at the fortress.

A little later, the lifeboat 'Wilhelm R Lundgren' from Rörö also appeared. It was probably the crew of the lifeboat that launched an inflatable boat with outboards. Two more people were rescued. This was another uncertain rescue mission, but it succeeded. However the captain did not want to go, and on the next attempt when the captain jumped overboard, they did not manage to save him. In total, 19 out of 20 people on board were rescued in this large operation, including a woman and three children.

The crew of the helicopter received great appreciation and also medals for their efforts. Göran believed, that the wind strength that the helicopter experienced was at least 50 m/s during the rescue operation, because at higher altitudes, the wind is much stronger. Göran does not know whether the boatmen who risked their lives in the hurricane got any appreciation.

The 'Agro Mayor', built in 1960 in steel, was 73 metres long, 11 metres wide and loaded with 675 tons of pulp was on its way from Mönsterås to Uddevalla, when it was hit by the storm. The remaining parts of the wreck are now between four and 20 metres deep.

Back to the introduction with Göran's camera. Despite the hurricane and the prevailing terrible situation, Göran had the presence of mind to use his camera to take photos. According to Göran, he then estimated that it was about 100 metres from the wave peak through the trough to the next peak and of course enormously high waves.

He writes that it took him a long time before it was possible to produce paper images. The pictures here show what it looked like, when the rescue was going on and how the ship was grounded on Grösslingen for a while before it breaks apart.

According to various sources on the internet, the hurricane in western Sweden in 1969 was an average of about 30-32 m/s, with gusts up to 40-45 m/s. The number of fatalities along the course of the storm was 6-11 people. Different information occurs, but it is clear that the 1969 hurricane is one of the worst in human memory.

The author's closing words

THIS BOOK IS not a critical journalistic work or a tribute to Göran. My work has been more about reproducing and showing from Göran's memory a large number of events and experiences, as well as all the different great achievements. My purpose has been to show the key moments, the talent and drive that led to Göran's success, both as a sailor and business leader. Of course, there were also major setbacks for Göran, both privately and as an entrepreneur, which have been omitted. The main purpose has been to make Göran remember and describe his sailing successes and the development of Marinex. As I see it, my task has been to try to convey a sailing and entrepreneurial life from Göran's perspective.

With a number of individual stories and narratives, other people have been helpful in describing what Göran first told me about, and to gain a better understanding, or get a different perspective of the people involved in the same events.

My conversations with Göran about his sailing and entrepreneurial life have covered more than 65 years. Once Göran has started, he has a fantastic memory (as in his sailing). If I have misunderstood different situations (despite research) or if Göran's memory has failed at some point, I hope that you, as a reader, will still enjoy a great deal of what has been written down. To the extent that the facts are not correct or misinterpreted, it is only me you can blame.

Thanks

I WOULD LIKE to extend a big thank you to Göran, who always stood up and contributed to me being able to write this book. To his wife, Ingrid, I would also like to express my thank for everything, from coffee and cake to helping with reading the text and making the necessary corrections, which hopefully made our work more readable.

To all those who have contributed factual information, some photos and friendly hospitality in various ways, I would like to express a big thank you. A special thank you, without diminishing any individual contribution, I would like to address Göran Kristensson, chairman of the Marstrand Local Heritage Society (Marstrands Hembygdsförening) and who has taken several new photos or scanned older photos for possible publication.

If there are comments or additions, the undersigned would be very grateful to receive these.

My email address is bjorn.ortendahl@gmail.com.

SOURCES, REFERENCES AND FACTS

I HAVE CHOSEN not to make a list of sources, but in the text I have tried to state different sources, which form the basis for what has been written. In cases where quotations or transcripts have been made, contacts have been made to ensure that publication may take place. In other respects, I refer to Göran's own extensive archive.

APPENDIX I

Summary of all of Göran's various great successes in sailing

DURING HIS ACTIVE years, Göran sailed both as helmsman and crew in a large number of different classes. Here are some classes besides Finn and OK Dinghy where Göran was active. In addition to sailing 5o5 in Hong Kong with Stefan Sjöström, he sailed the 5o5 World Championship in Marstrand in 1974. Here Göran was a crew and Björn Arnesson a helmsman. They took a bronze medal in this event and it was the first time that Swedes won a medal in this class. He also sailed a European Championship in the Star boat in Gottskär. Göran was the crew and Thomas Lundqvist the helmsman. Thomas was also a really good Finn sailor and as a 22-year-old in 1969, he won the Finn Gold Cup in Bermuda. Göran has also sailed in other keelboats. With Erik 'Kicken' Larsson's folk boat, Göran as helmsman and crew Hans Larsson and Richard Josefsson took second place at the Swedish Championship on Lake Vättern.

In the J-24 class Leif Qvint won the first unofficial Swedish Championship in Marstrand with Göran as skipper. Göran successfully sailed a Maxi 77 with Lennart Claesson (Kullbo). Göran has also had time for ocean racing. As early as 1964, some Marstrand guys, Gunnar and Sture Lückner, Göran and Sture Andersson, and Bertil Nicander, as well as Commander Krusell got to try ocean racing together with Sven Frisell, a summer resident at Backudden, in his two-masted boat 'Kay'. Sven Frisell's regular summer employee guest Stig Andreasson was there as usual. This was the beginning for several, then young, Marstrand boys who continued to sail at sea at a high level for a large number of years.

APPENDIX II

Weather Changes, Tactics and Currents

FOR SAILORS OF all ages

1. CHECK IF there is high pressure, about 1020 hPa (hectopascal) in Iceland. Then there will be poor weather on the Swedish west coast. If the pressure is low in Iceland, below 1000 hPa, then the weather is fine on the Swedish West Coast. In Iceland you can experience four-seasons in one day.

2. IF YOU are in at sea and the barometer drops four (4) hPa within an hour, take the fastest route to a safe harbour. Storms are approaching – the sea will become turbulent and dangerous.

3. IN THE middle of the Marstrandsfjord, a large ring of current flows, within a line from Engelsmannen-Kråkorna towards Skallen's lighthouse. When sailing there, try to take advantage of the current. Head towards Pater Noster, then when halfway take a course towards Skäreläje hake. Then a new course towards Åstol, and when halfway take a new course towards Isacbåden then to Engelsmannen. (This describes how the current runs on the Marstrandsfjorden.) Hook on to the 'power wheel' (This is an advice to follow the current while racing on the Marstrandsfjorden. The current behaves like a wheel and is called the 'power wheel' in this text). In the evening when the wind has calmed down, the 'wheel' spins (the current turns around), and is affected by the offshore north or south running current (the Norwegian current), which splits at Hätteberget and partly flows towards Åstol and Södra Åstol and towards Hakefjorden to Uddevalla.

4. IF THERE is high tide in Byfjorden / Gustafsberg, the water is pushed out west along the east and west edges. It flows out towards Engelsmannen - Kråkorna and also along the skerries out to Pater Noster. (To interpret this description, use nautical chart 9321, special chart Marstrand.)

5. SAILING ON a close reach on the Marstrandsfjord, say a port tack towards Truskär and about 5-7 m/s, if there is a boat, a bit in front of you and it suddenly falls off 5-10°, you may think that the wind is heading.

6. NO, IT is because the current is strong. Continue sailing your course, you are in the right current channel - you are not disturbed by the boat in front. This tactic is good in other waters such as the Sound, Malmö and Copenhagen.

7. WHEREVER, YOU sail on the Marstrandsfjord, look for any fishing gear, such as buoys. Check the current around these. Check compass heading how the current 'flows'.

8. START: IF you decided to go for a windward start, (on starboard) but got a safe start right behind first line of boats at the windward starting vessel, there's a good chance that you can tack to port after about 50 metres. Then tack back to starboard and now you may have clear air.

9. WINDS FROM the sea rarely have large shifts, they are often small and difficult to detect. It is very important to also consider the small current that may be in the water (or stronger as before).

10. WINDS FROM the land are usually quite shifty, which require tacking and thus profiting from the changing wind.

11. CREW ON board a racing boat must move smoothly, i.e. move with the utmost care.

12. SOMEONE IN the crew should keep an eye astern and assess drift against the last rounded mark.

13. GROUND PLANES (really small islands that are barely seen above the water), which are visible, can be a good point of reference for determining your position.

14. AN EXCELLENT training exercise is to sail on different lakes and concentrate on handling wind shifts.

15. GÖRAN SAYS he has sailed on lakes in Sweden, Germany, Belgium, Holland, France, Norway and Canada. "These different places have given me a lot of experience to interpret different winds and waves."

16. IF YOU sail on the sea and happen to be against the current, on both sides of the large current there is usually a counter-current running in the opposite direction.

17. TO TEST the above, head to Bäveån in Uddevalla, near the church. There you can see strong current in the middle and on both sides of it there are currents running the opposite way (works just as well with any other flowing water).

18. FOR LONGER voyages in the southern hemisphere, study literature and manuals about the winds and currents that will prevail along the route you intend to sail.

19. IF YOU want to understand currents, extra carefully, in winter if the sea has been icy and now instead begin to consist of loose ice floes, do the following: Go up to a high place (where you can see the ice floes from above) and follow their path, which is then most affected of prevailing currents. A good place for this, regarding Marstrand and Hakefjorden is on Koön above the treatment plant (the 'black trail' road on Koön). This possibility is now very limited as we have not had any real ice in winter for many years. In the 1950s and 1960s it was much more common.

20. A SIMPLE tool for quick mapping of the direction of the current: use a sheet from a newspaper and cut into approx. 12 x 5 cm pieces, throw in and read the strength of the current.

21. IF DANGER is approaching, such as risk of thunderstorms – prepare the crew- set small sails, reef or remove mainsail and foresail before thunderstorms approach.

22. WHEN SAILING or racing on the Marstrandsfjord, the thunderstorms mostly come in from the south-east. As it gets closer, it becomes an easterly direction. If the gusts, and the thunderclaps, are getting stronger, and the wind is increasing, a lot of rain is coming. Thunderstorms that can be up to 20 m/s. Suddenly the wind drops to total calm. Then after that, the new winds usually come from Rönnängsberget, where racers can find gaps with new winds though these winds are very shifty, which could be useful.

23. SOLAR WINDS are interesting. They start from the east and arrive at about 06.00 and then shift to a southerly direction. When the evening breeze has subsided, it will be calm at night from 24.00 to 0500-0600, when the morning breeze starts. Racing usually starts at 10.00, but then the wind stops, which sometimes means that the race is postponed while waiting for new stable winds.

24. SEA BREEZE is a nice form of wind. It starts at about 15.00 time and increases, to about 7-8 m/s; at dusk it decreases.

25. DIFFERENT WEATHER conditions (thunder, sea breeze, solar winds, etc.) can be very local. If you race at home, knowledge and experience from these local 'conditions' can be the basis for achieving better results.

26. A FUN exercise for the little ones to start understanding how winds change direction. Children can stick a stick in the ground with a light yarn on top and read with the help of a small compass how the wind shifts.

SWEDISH SAILING HALL OF FAME

AFTER THE FIRST Swedish edition of this book was printed, Göran Andersson was elected to the Swedish Sailing Hall of Fame, in 2019.

The following motivation for the appointment has been provided by the Swedish Sailing Association:

Motivation: Member number twelve in the Swedish Sailing Hall of Fame was born in Lysekil in 1939 and represented Marstrand's SS when he sailed the Finn in the 1960 Olympics.

But it was in the OK Dinghy that he reaped his greatest successes with, among other things, two World Championship golds (1965 and 1966) when the OK Dinghy was the world's largest one-man dinghy class.

During the 1960s and 1970s, this year's winner was one of the world's leading sailmakers, mast manufacturers and boat builders. Anyone who wanted success on the racing courses in OK Dinghy and Finn used sails from Marinex – the company he started in the early 1960s.

Photo by Daniel Stenholm

POSTSCRIPT
BY THE PUBLISHER

IN 2020, GÖRAN ANDERSSON WAS inducted into the OK Dinghy Hall of Fame. It was intended to happen during the OK Dinghy World Championship, in Marstrand in August 2020, but the COVID-19 pandemic caused the regatta to be cancelled. However the induction of Göran into the Hall of Fame went ahead in June with a quiet meeting at his home on Tjörn.

Göran wrote afterwards:

"What an amazing honour to be elected into the hall of fame. I feel extremely honoured and fortunate to be the recipient of such a precious title when looking back at the time at sea. I share this legacy with my family and I will celebrate this honour with my fellow sailors.

It is also my hope that this prize will create a spirit and genuine passion for our sport, that will live on for generations of sailors to come.

This award signifies the trust and belief of my peers in me and my abilities, without whom I would not have come as far as I have.

There are many people I would like to express my gratitude towards, some who are sadly no longer with us, but they will all be remembered with reverence."

THE PUBLISHER WOULD like to thank and acknowledge the assistance of Björn Örtendahl, the author; Göran Kristensson, the Chairman of Marstrand Local Heritage Society; and Jonas Börjesson, Vice President of the OK Dinghy International Association with their assistance in translating the Swedish edition. Without their combined help, this English edition would not have been possible.

GÖRAN ANDERSSON DIED on November 18, 2020 a few weeks before this edition was published.

Göran Andersson with the OKDIA Hall of Fame award • Photo: Jonas Börjesson

www.ingramcontent.com/pod-product-compliance
Lightning Source LLC
Chambersburg PA
CBHW071533080526
44588CB00011B/1657